THE LIGHTING BOOK

Cover photo: Sintesi floor lamp, designed by Ernesto Gismondi for Artemide. Courtesy of Artemide Inc., New York.

THE
LIGHTING

BOOK by Martin Greif

A BUYER'S GUIDE TO LOCATING ALMOST EVERY KIND OF LIGHTING DEVICE

THE MAIN STREET PRESS • PITTSTOWN, NEW JERSEY

For Ilene and Irwin Hochberg.
Ex luce lucellum.

First edition 1986

All rights reserved
Copyright © 1986 by The Main Street Press

Published by
The Main Street Press
William Case House
Pittstown, New Jersey 08867

Published simultaneously in Canada by
Methuen Publications
2330 Midland Avenue
Agincourt, Ontario M1S 1P7

Printed in the United States of America

Library of Congress Cataloging-in-Publication Data

Greif, Martin.
   The lighting book.

   1. Electric lamps—Catalogs. I. Title.
TK4310.G73 1985   621.32′2′029473   85-24199
ISBN 0-915590-81-6
ISBN 0-915590-82-4 (pbk.)

Contents

Intro-
duction

This book is for anyone in pursuit of a simple, well-proportioned lighting fixture who has ever stumbled into that contemporary chamber of horrors called a lighting shop. If you've discovered in the midst of that jumble of cheap glass and missshapen metal that all you've ever come home with was a stiff neck, then *The Lighting Book* is certainly for you: Almost none of the 1,000 fixtures illustrated in its pages can be found in the conventional lighting store.

The Lighting Book is a comprehensive guide to locating almost every kind of lighting device, both indoor and out. It covers antique, reproduction, and contemporary lighting fixtures from 18th-century lanterns and chandeliers to Victorian gaslights and ultramodern Italian fixtures that represent the ultimate in space-age design. Its many selections enable you to choose from scores of lighting suppliers nationwide and from hundreds of different types of fixtures, including table lamps, track lighting, outdoor fixtures, wall sconces, floor lamps, ceiling fixtures, antique lighting devices, post lights, and hanging lamps among many others.

If your decorating scheme requires period fixtures, *The Lighting Book* includes recommended devices from candlesticks and candlestands to betty, gas, kerosene, and early electric lamps. If interested in modern design, you'll discover lighting fixtures that are decorative elements in themselves, classic forms fabricated in up-to-the-minute materials. Energy-saving innovations—fluorescent fixtures and halogen and mercury-vapor lamps—are covered as are suppliers of accessories and other specialties. Addresses and telephone numbers of suppliers are listed for all fixtures illustrated. If a particular model interests you, all you have to do is consult the List of Suppliers at the end of the book for the maker's address and number. Many manufacturers will let you know where you can purchase their fixtures locally; others will ship you lighting fixtures directly from their workshops and showrooms.

In compiling *The Lighting Book,* I have had the assistance of several colleagues whose contributions I gladly acknowledge. Without Liz Rolfe's organizational wizardry, Vicki Brooks's verbal prestidigitation, and Frank Mahood's and John Fox's design skills, this book would still be an unrealized idea in the head of its author.

1.
Period Lighting

The problem in selecting lighting fixtures for old houses or for modern spaces decorated in a period style is not the limit of choices, but the virtually endless possibilities. Antique fixtures are available, newly wired and restored. Craftsmen are turning out high-quality handmade devices taken from many periods. There is also an enormous market in machine-tooled reproduction fixtures. "Reproduction" does not necessarily mean shoddy materials and tacky designs. Many companies produce fixtures from such top-quality materials as solid brass, and with such elegant appointments as etched ruby-glass shades or mirrored reflectors.

There are probably some people who can cook in a kitchen lit by a flickering candle in a tin sconce, but the truth is that if electricity had been harnessed at the time, the Colonists would have used it. With the availability of quality fixtures today, there is no need to sacrifice convenience for historical authenticity down to the stub of a candle. A Victorian dining room can be outfitted with a fully wired, handsome brass gasolier or a table lamp with a fringed silk lampshade. Graceful, hand-forged iron or pewter wall sconces are eminently suitable for 18th-century rooms. And outdoor areas can be lit in a variety of imaginative ways, most notably with glass and metal lanterns designed to be hung, wall-mounted, or affixed to a post.

An important consideration in choosing lighting is the space and the manner in which it will be used. Candle sconces offer lively light in a dining room, until they drip wax on the random-width floorboards, overturn suddenly, or become objects of fascination to a child. Such fixtures can be fitted with electric candles and still be effective.

Hallways are often suitable for simple hanging fixtures. They are less elaborate than chandeliers and are available in a variety of period styles. Good reading lights are harder to come by, but there are simple reproduction wrought-iron table lamps modeled after candlestands or electrified candlestands themselves that are perfectly suitable in design and function.

The pages of this chapter offer many sources for reproduction and antique fixtures to satisfy both the requirements of modern lighting and the harmony of period decor.

Opposite page: Two examples of fine handmade tin fixtures from Lt. Moses Willard—a pentagon lantern and a round pan sconce.

9

Antique Lighting Fixtures

There was a time when every junkyard had its share of
gasoliers and early electric light fixtures, when only "Early
American" devices had any value at all to collectors. But that
time has long passed. The Victorian period is now far enough
away in time to be newly appreciated, and even fixtures of the
1920s and the Depression years command astonishing prices
today. Although the demand for authentic period lighting
devices far exceeds the supply, good pieces are readily
available in the marketplace if you happen to have both the
pocket for the real thing and the insider's knowledge of where
to find the best sources of supply. Descriptions of some of the
most reputable dealers follow.

1-3. Specializing in original gas
chandeliers, wall sconces, and table
lamps from the period 1850 to
1887, **Stanley Galleries** also main-
tains a large stock of early electric
fixtures, including many in the Arts
and Crafts and Art Deco styles.
The inventory of fine table lamps
always includes several signed Tiffany lamps to highlight the group.
The firm will gladly suggest the
correct antique fixture for your
needs if you delineate in writing the
size and function of the room to be
illuminated and the period of its
decor. **4.** At **Yankee Craftsman**, Bill
Sweeney and his three sons take
such pride in restoring period fixtures and in providing custom

1

2

3

4

5

6

7

8

9

designs that their shop has taken on the ambience of the late-19th century, a period they obviously love. Yankee Craftsman stocks a large inventory of antique fixtures; if you're looking for a specific type that the Sweeneys might have, they will send a photograph and information at no charge. **5. Price Glover Incorporated** sells only the finest English antiques, including rare brass lighting fixtures of the 18th century. Shown here is a triple sconce, so handsome that the original has been selected for reproduction by the firm (see p. 53). **6-7. London Venturers** is committed to antique lighting, proud of the distinction of having been the first dealer in North America to offer catalogue sales of restored fixtures. The antiques shown testify to the magic which skillful restoration can bring to dusty glass and tarnished brass. **8-9.** In addition to maintaining a stock of restored antique lighting devices, Barry Hauptman's **Authentic Lighting** offers a variety of services. The firm will restore and finish fixtures from any period from Victorian gasoliers to Art Deco pendants and can reproduce a fixture from an original, photo, or blueprint you supply.

1

2

3

1, 4. Although **Greg's Antique Lighting** specializes in the very finest Victorian fixtures, painstakingly restored and wired for modern use, later lighting fixtures through the Art Deco period are also represented. Greg Davidson's collection, the largest on the West Coast, also includes table lamps by Handel, Bradley and Hubbard, and Pairpoint. And, if you're seeking a replacement shade, Greg's has assembled a comprehensive stock of antique glass shades—art glass, pressed, etched, or cut—by such famous makers as Steuben, Loetz, and Quezal. The firm will send photographs of suitable fixtures in response to specific inquiries received by mail or telephone.

2-3, 5. The St. Louis warehouse of **Art Directions** contains a large collection of architectural antiques, including brass, bronze, and crystal lighting fixtures from the Victorian through the Art Deco periods and ranging in size from the residential to the institutional. The firm is capable of reproducing any antique fixture to order and is in the process of creating a standard line of reproductions from the varied treasures in its large inventory.

4

5

6, 8-9. Materials Unlimited is a virtual shopping center for lovers of period decor. Among the splendid architectural antiques and furnishings to be found here is a wide collection of original lighting fixtures, from candelabras and gasoliers to the most fanciful early electric chandeliers. Among the holdings are many art glass lamps by Tiffany, Handel, and Quezal. A majority of the hundreds of fixtures on display are fully restored and ready for installation. Fixtures can be modified to suit ceiling heights, and they can be duplicated by request in the company's extensive workshops. **7. Roy Electric Co.** stocks a large inventory of Victorian and turn-of-the-century gas and electric fixtures, parts, lamp bases, and virtually anything pertaining to old lighting fixtures. It can also turn the old wreck you've been been keeping in the attic into a functioning beauty since it fully repairs, restores, refinishes, casts, plates, bends, polishes, lacquers, and rewires old fixtures as well.

Other reliable suppliers of antique lighting fixtures include: **Brass Light of Historic Walker's Point, Citybarn Antiques, City Lights, Half-Moon Antiques,** and **Turn of the Century Lighting** (see List of Suppliers for details).

6

7

8

9

Candleholders

1

The history of the candle is steeped in antiquity, immortalized in literature, poetry, and song. This simple lighting device has played an important part in nearly every religion, and its soft yellow light yields a romantic atmosphere to our homes today. Romantic as candlelight may be, it performed a serious and vital role in early American life. Unlike the lamp which needs care in the supply of fuel and adjustment of the wick, the candle is a self-contained lighting unit, clean and safe, and has required little or no attention from the user since 1825 when the introduction of the braided wick eliminated the need for snuffing. The very utility of this simple lighting device seems both to have inspired the design of inventive holders throughout the centuries and to have assured its continued use for romantic effect in the modern age. Although department stores and catalogue houses offer a variety of candleholders, almost none of their wares is suitable for the period interior. The many candle-burning devices shown on the following pages are highly recommended. Each is a traditional form and illustrative of the fine reproduction work being done today by period lighting experts.

When it comes to early Colonial lighting devices, no one surpasses **Hurley Patentee Lighting.** The originals of all Hurley fixtures are present in museums and private collections throughout North America. Each piece of wood or metal used in a Hurley reproduction is hand-crafted in the manner of the Colonial period which the piece represents. The only modification of the original is in electrifying the fixture for contemporary use. Illustrated here and on the following page is a sampling of the large collection of Hurley devices from the earliest period of the American Colonies:

1. Early iron candleholders were frequently equipped with push-up levers to raise and expel tapers from the holders. Hurley's simple push-up candleholders (left) are available in electrified and non-electrified models, in 10″ and 7″ heights. Also pictured are 14″ and 10″ ladderback candleholders, so-called because of a lip for hooking over the back slat of a chair to facilitate reading or sewing. Occasionally used for scratching the backs of pigs, the device was popularly known as a "hogscraper." **2.** This 17th-century scissors rushlight was meant to hold a reed soaked in fat or, for the wealthy, a candle. Hurley's 16″-high reproduction holds a candle socket.

2

3

4

5

6

3. The 5″-high candleholder on the left has a cone base with a punched design and a large drip saucer. Pictured in the center is a simple tin chamberstick, 5″ wide, meant originally to light the way to bed. The coil-base holder on the right is made of iron and tin and stands 9″ high. **4.** Designed with handsome straight and curved lines, this three-light iron table stand is 14″ high and 13″ wide. **5.** A good example of 18th-century ingenuity, this 12″-high iron barrel holder was meant to be hooked over a barrel or a chair slat. Today it would look just fine set proudly on a table. **6.** In primitive Betty lamps, a flame issues from a wick inserted in an oil-filled cup. **Hurley** handcrafts authentic models fueled with oil and others equipped to hold candles.

1

1. Baldwin Giftware's sparkling candelabra, reproduced from originals in American museums, dramatically enliven the dining table or sideboard. Each arm is delicately articulated with a quality of detail and finish that suggests the essence of the 18th century. The manufacturer offers many models, each bearing the seal of the museum housing the original. Shown is model FP 7407. For an even more sumptuous look, add Baldwin's adaptors and glass globes to create a cluster of hurricane lighting. **2.** This fine reproduction of an 18th-century candlestick stands 8″ tall and is available in heavy polished brass from **Period Furniture Hardware Co. 3.** Available in a range of designs and sizes, candlesticks from **Baldwin Giftware** are perfect used singly for a soft, warm accent or grouped together for a dazzling candlelit display. Shown here are only three models (FP 7300, FP 7310, and FP 7320) of the scores offered, each reproduced from museum originals. **4.** These reproductions of very early, rare, turned-brass candlesticks are authentic in every detail. Produced by **Hurley Patentee Lighting**, they are available in 7″ and 5″ (with bobeche) models. **5-7.** Three additional examples of brass candlesticks from **Period Furniture Hardware:** model FP 7022 (6¾″ high), model FP 7026 (8½″ high), and model FP 7008 (9¾″ high). Each is wrought of antique-finished brass.

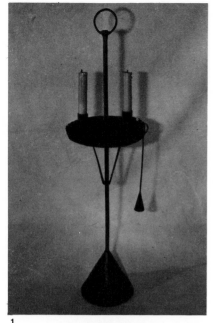

1

2

3

4

Hurley Patentee Lighting is justly famous for its faithful reproductions of 17th- and 18th-century lighting devices. Shown here is only a small selection of Hurley's early candleholders and other primitive fixtures. **1.** This early tin table stand with weighted cone base and round drip plate stands 30″ high and holds two tapers. **2.** The saucer above this tin lodging-room lamp originally held sweet herbs to con-

ceal the odor of burning oil. Now the 9″-high, 14″-long lamp is equipped to hold candles. **3.** This 22″-tall tin and iron table stand features a large surface for greater reflection of candlelight. **4.** Functional and beautiful, this tin candleholder has a long handle for carrying and a convenient drip pan. It can be placed on a table or hung when not in use. *Opposite page:* **5.** This electrified iron and brass

late-18th-century desk lamp, 28″ high, is also available in single light (see illustration **8**) and all-iron models. **6.** Electrified single-light brass desk lamp, 21″ high. The front holds lamp oil for burning during power failures. **7.** This 32″-high shaded table lamp is available with or without electrical wiring.

5

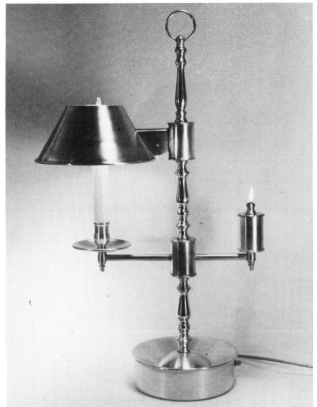

6

7

8

1. The Manor floor lamp by **Hurley Patentee Lighting** is available electrified or as a candleholder. 65″ high. **2.** Practical and handsome patio lamps by **The Washington Copper Works** won't blow out. Available with or without handles. 10″ high. **3.** An electrified 18th-century candlestand is an ideal reading lamp. The harp moves up and down on its wrought-iron spindle and turns a full 360°. The 52″-high lamp by **The Essex Forge** includes a nubby burlap shade. **4.** The Tollgate Hill, an 11″-high electrified candlestand suitable for end table or hall table by **The Washington Copper Works.** *Opposite page:* **5.** A selection of 18th-century lamps with hurricane globes by **Baldwin Giftware.** Shown, left to right, are models 7430, 7416, 7500, and 7411, each a museum replica.

2

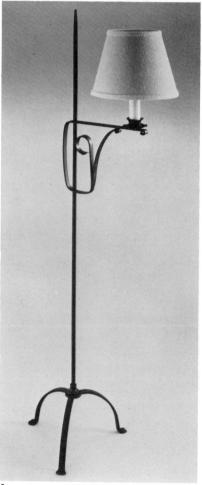

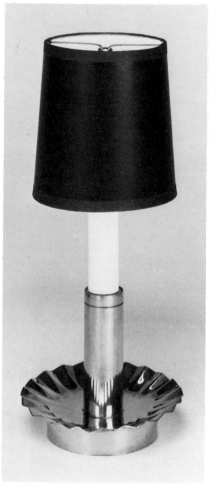

1

3

4

Simple Metal Chandeliers

Chandeliers are often used for the wrong reason—to make fancy what was originally simple. While it's true that handsome hanging fixtures of brass and pewter were used in Colonial America, most of them were imported from the foundries of England and were intended for churches, town halls, and the homes of the very wealthy. In most Colonial houses, however, the chandelier was little more than a simple form of hanging light, usually made of wood or tin or hand-wrought iron. Not until the 19th century, and well into it, could any sizable number of people afford to use more elaborate fixtures employing crystal or etched glass. The simplest Colonial chandeliers, as seen in these pages, were masterpieces of the metalworker's art. Happily, they are readily reproduced by a small band of dedicated artisans for today's period home.

2

1

3

1. Electrified **Gates Moore** chandelier with hand-painted wooden center and eight metal arms with hand-crimped bobeches. Perfectly authentic in every detail. 24″ wide, 10″ high. **2.** An example of the exquisite period lighting fixtures that can be made to order at Ned James's **Mill River Hammerworks,** experts in both period and contemporary metalwork. Commissions accepted from both individuals and institutions.

Opposite page: **3.** The Bookbinder Series, three electrified models of early tavern lights, in black-finished steel, by **Newstamp Lighting Co.** *This page:* **4.** A hand-forged iron chandelier by **Kayne & Son Custom Forged Hardware.** All period lighting fixtures by Steve Kayne are made on commission from your sketch or description. As Mr. Kayne writes, "tell us your needs and we will produce a custom product to meet them." **5.** Lighting by **Hammerworks** hand-forges this graceful 18th-century chandelier in a variety of antique finishes. Also made in four- and five-arm models, in sizes from 21″ to 26″ wide and 13″ high. **6.** **Hurley Patentee Lighting**'s three-lamp chandelier is a reproduction of a refined late-18th-century original. It is 23″ high and 17″ wide and is also available in a four-arm model. **7-8.** Also by **Hurley Patentee Lighting** are this iron-ring chandelier, a rare design in hand-forged iron (20″ high, 14″ wide) and the bird-hook chandelier, once used in formal Colonial homes (24″ high, 10″ wide).

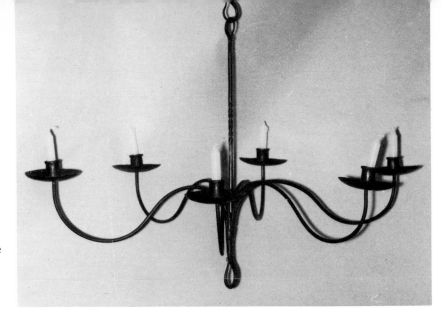

4

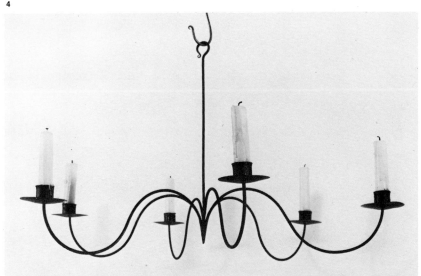

5

6

7

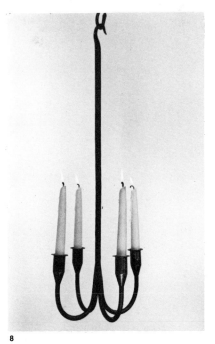

8

1

Wood and Metal Chandeliers

"Lighting the darkness," write Stephen and Carolyn Waligur-ski, "began with fire. To the colonial three centuries ago, this meant the fireplace, the torch, and the Betty lamp. In the 17th century, candles were a luxury and used only on special occasions. Gradually, more candles were used until simple fixtures became functional works of art culminating in the chandelier." What makes the late-Colonial and early Federal wood and metal chandelier so appealing today is its spacious airiness, its graceful simplicity that is a natural concomitant of well-proportioned, well-turned wooden center posts and spidery tin or copper or iron candle-bearing arms. Scores of wood and metal chandeliers, reproduced from originals in museums and private collections, are made by hand today. Among the best are the fixtures shown here and on the pages following.

Period chandeliers from **Lt. Moses Willard & Company** are entirely handmade and authentic in every detail. *Opposite page:* **1.** Model 4163 is the graceful centerpiece of a Colonial dining room. Available electrified or with candleholders, the chandelier can be made with either ten or twelve arms. 30″ wide, 25″ high. **2.** The Drake chandelier, with painted or stained wooden center, has six tin arms. 20″ wide, 15″ high. **3.** The Browne chandelier, with wood center turning, has six flat distressed tin arms. 24″ wide, 12″ high. **4.** The Brewton chandelier, modeled on an original in Historic Charleston, is available in four different models. The model shown has eight brass arms. 24″ wide, 14″ high. **5.** Model 4413, electrified or fitted for candles, comes with either six or eight arms. 24″ wide, 22″ high.

2

3

4

5

1. **Authentic Designs** is dedicated to re-creating classic lighting fixtures of exceptional quality. Typical of the firm's fine work is model CH-109, a perfectly proportioned chandelier, 22½″ wide and 22½″ high. 2. In **Hurley Patentee Lighting**'s nine-arm Massachusetts Tavern chandelier, two levels of lights are intermingled on one tier (three over six), an outstanding example of Colonial design ingenuity. 34″ wide, 23″ high. 3. **Hurley**'s five-arm Rolling Pin chandelier, based on a Virginia original, is 24″ wide and 17″ high. 4. **Lt. Moses Willard & Company** handcrafts this five-arm chandelier with large drip plates (#4433) in electrified and non-electrified models. Also available with four arms. 13½″ wide, 9″ high.

1

2

4

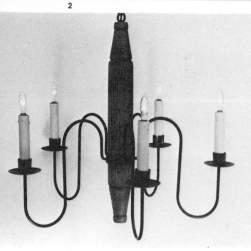

3

5

6

Opposite page: **5. Hurley Patentee Lighting**'s Meeting House chandelier is Shaker in inspiration. With thirteen gently curved arms, the fixture measures 44″ wide and 20″ high (the dimensions of the original) or can be made to your specifications. *This page:* **6. Gates Moore** hand-produces this fine chandelier in four different sizes, ranging in width from 29″ to 48″ and including as many as twenty curving arms (ten over ten). The model shown (#32) measures 40″ wide and 28″ high and is painted in Colonial red or green or to match your own color sample. **7.** Made entirely by hand from solid maple and custom metal, **Authentic Design**'s twelve-arm chandelier (CH-102) measures 22″ wide and 26½″ high. **8.** Boasting twenty-four arms with hand-crimped bobeches on three levels, this lovely fixture (#4111) from **Lt. Moses Willard & Company** is available in electrified and non-electrified models and is 36″ wide and 23½″ high. An exquisite piece of hand work, the wood and metal chandelier demonstrates why the firm likes to call itself (in the old style) "tinkers and whittlers."

8

7

There's a fine line separating whimsy from kitsch. And the people at **Lt. Moses Willard** are decidedly on the side of the angels—and apparently the turkeys, and horses, and apples. Tin folk art figures adorn a wide and varied line of wood and metal chandeliers handcrafted by this Ohio firm, three of which are illustrated here. **1.** The Smokebell Turkey Chandelier is 36″ wide and 20″ high and is available in models with ten or twelve arms, each of which supports a cutout turkey on its upward curve. Tin smokebells are mounted atop the fixture, and the base of the center turning is carved in a pineapple pattern. This chandelier is also available without the smokebells. **2.** The Animal Chandelier comes in one model only and measures 24″ wide and 16″ high. Six folk art animals grace the fixture, one per arm—a lamb, hen, rooster, pig, cow, and horse. **3.** The Apple Chandelier is 32″ wide and 12″ high, with a wood apple-shaped turning painted (what else?) apple red with green highlights. Green tin leaves accent the top of the turning and five distressed tin arms complete the whimsical lighting fixture. For those whose taste runs to other fruits, Lt. Moses Willard offers wonderful folk art chandeliers in the shape of pineapples, pears, strawberries, watermelons, and even acorns—a veritable cornucopia for the country dining room. With the exception of the watermelon, each shape is also available in a matching wall sconce.

1

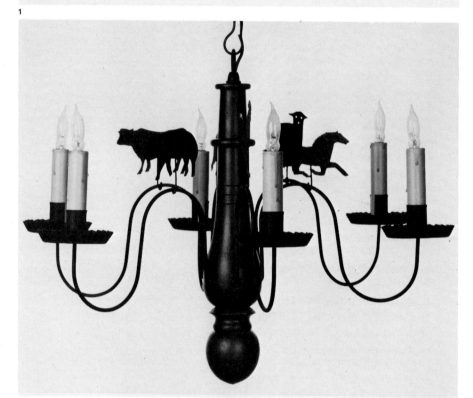

2

3

If you've ever wondered why many Colonial-style reproduction chandeliers look unnatural and out of proportion, take a closer look at the type of metal tubing used. In many cases fat tubing is utilized for convenience since it's easier to thread wiring through a wide aperture than a thin one. At **Authentic Designs,** Dan Krauss doesn't skimp on authenticity. He believes that if the wire doesn't fit, don't alter the fixture—find a thinner wire. Attention to such details makes the fixtures produced in this workshop almost unique. No brass plating is used; no modern lacquers or preservatives are allowed to interfere with the natural aging process of the metal. In addition, a great deal of research goes into the design of these chandeliers before their fabrication in Authentic's reconstructed antique mill. The graceful curves of the brass arms are realized by using methods employed two centuries ago.

Shown here are only a few of the many chandeliers offered by Authentic Designs. **4.** CH-188 is 21″ wide and 9½″ high. **5.** CH-400 is 20″ wide and 16″ high. **6.** CH-155, one of several models with reflectors, is 12½″ wide and 17½″ high. **7.** CH-149 is 23″ wide and 9½″ high. **8.** CH-170 is 21″ wide and 13½″ high. **9.** CH-213 is 26″ wide and 22″ high. These Colonial-style chandeliers have been electrified, but for lovers of the truly authentic—like Krauss—they are also available unwired.

4

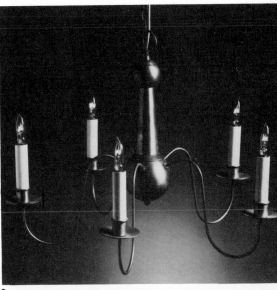

5

6

7

8

9

Tin Chandeliers

The Reverend William Bentley of Salem commented, in 1801, on visiting the church at Exeter, New Hampshire: "I observed a chandelier in this old building which is a very rare thing in America." By the second decade of the 19th century, however, that rare household commodity—the chandelier—was becoming increasingly less rare. New England excelled in making handsome devices for holding candles. The woodturner and woodcarver had a hand in the making of chandeliers, but the tinsmith's contribution was even more superb. Subtle in line and proportion, tin chandeliers were devised in almost every design that lent itself to hammer and solder. On this page and others following are examples of classic early American tin fixtures reproduced with excellence by today's lighting artisans.

3

4

5

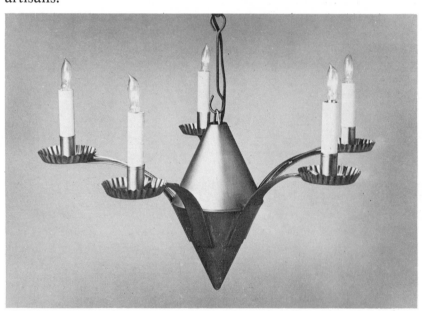

1

2

1. **Lt. Moses Willard**'s model #4241 has five arms and measures 22″ wide and 12″ high. It is also available with six arms and with and without electrification. 2. The original of The Deerfield chandelier by **The Essex Forge** hangs in the Frary Tavern in historic Deerfield. Electrified or with holders for candles, the chandelier, one of many tin fixtures by this well-known firm, measures 30″ wide and 14″ high.

Opposite page: **3.** Eight-arm chandelier by **Gates Moore.** Available in several finishes, including distressed tin. 20″ wide, 11″ high. **4.** Doubledecker chandelier by **Gates Moore.** Available with four arms over eight, as shown, or with five arms over ten. 24″ wide, 15″ high. (The larger model is 34″ wide.) **5. Lt. Moses Willard**'s model #4342. Available with five or six arms, electrified or with candle sockets. 20½″ wide, 14½″ high. *This page:* **6.** The Wareham chandelier by **The Essex Forge.** Central core of electrified model has a downlight for soft illumination below. Also available, as shown, with candle-holders. 26″ wide, 12″ high. **8. Lt. Moses Willard**'s model #4221 is shown to advantage in a period room. It is made with either six or eight arms, either electrified or non-electrified. 24″ wide, 16″ high.

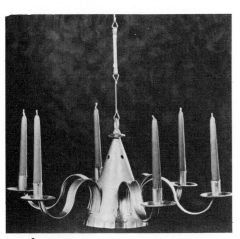

6

7

8

1

2

3

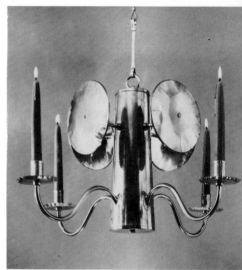

4

5

Opposite page: **1. Lt. Moses Willard**'s model #4091 presents still another variation on the almost limitless possibilities of early American tinkering. Bands of tin, soldered in graceful shapes, come together in a simple chandelier of unusual grace. The five-arm fixture is available in electrified or candleholding models and measures 21″ wide and 18½″ high. **2. Hurley Patentee Lighting** handcrafts this striking chandelier dubbed The Flowing Fountain. Twelve tapered branches flow from a 10″ curved center plate of iron and tin. It measures 36″ wide and 20″ high. An eight-arm model, also available, is 28″ wide and 18″ high. **3.** The primitive two-tier chandelier, by **Hurley Patentee Lighting,** is a reproduction of an early nine-light fixture of tin. Like other Hurley fixtures, it is authentic in every detail. 26″ wide, 19″ high. **4.** The original of **The Essex Forge**'s New Bedford Whaler chandelier hung in the captain's cabin of a Massachusetts whaling vessel. The unique four-arm chandelier is available electrified or with candleholders. 24″ wide, 14″ high. **5.** The New Bedford Whaler, electrified. *This page:* **6.** In this tin chandelier by **Shaker Workshops**, the geometric form of the double cone contrasts well with the six free-curving arms. 24″ wide, 16″ high. **7. The Saltbox** offers over 250 styles of authentic early American lighting, one of which, the exquisitely simple tavern chandelier, is pictured here in a period setting. 28″ wide, 18″ high. **8. Hurley Patentee Lighting**'s primitive five-branch chandelier is a reproduction of an early tin fixture with a pierced design in the base. 20″ wide, 14″ high.

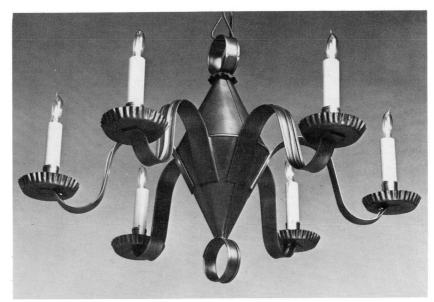

6

7

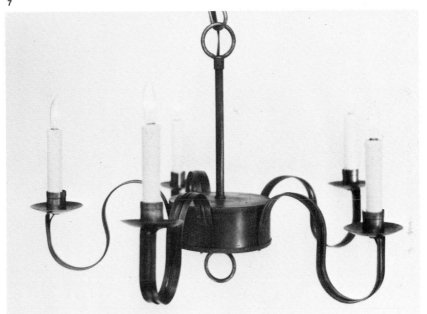

8

Pierced Tin Chandeliers

The art of piercing tin in decorative designs originally served a functional purpose. Tin lanterns, for example, were pierced to allow beams of light to penetrate the darkness, and pie safes were pierced for the circulation of air. But, as the chandeliers on these pages attest, tin piercing also existed for its own sake—for sheer beauty.

1. Lt. Moses Willard's handsome model #4500 is made with four or five candle-bearing arms. In both, the top cylinder is electrified for subtle downlighting. The pierced tin chandelier measures 25″ wide and 25″ high.

1

2

3

4

5

6

2. Lt. Moses Willard's model #4400 is available both electrified and non-electrified and with either six or eight arms. On the models with candle-bearing arms, the center cone is electrified, allowing light to shine through the pierced-tin pattern. 24″ wide, 17″ high. **3.** The Salisbury, by **The Essex Forge**, is a delightful dining room centerpiece. The central double cone, with hundreds of hand-punched perforations, conceals a light within. The fixture is available electrified only. 26″ wide, 16″ high. **4.** No such fixture as a pierced-tin Tiffany-style shade with downlight ever existed in the past, but for a country kitchen it might provide just the right tone of civilized rusticity. Made by **Lt. Moses Willard**, it measures 15″ wide and 12″ high. **5. Hurley Patentee Lighting**'s pierced-lantern chandelier contains a downlight in the lantern and has electrified or candle-bearing arms. 24″ wide, 14″ high. **6. Hurley**'s charming barnyard chandelier has a downlight in the lantern and arms either wired or candle-bearing. If ducks don't suit you, Hurley offers a menagerie of fourteen animals to choose from. 24″ wide, 16″ high.

Brass Chandeliers

The chandelier that is usually thought of as quintessentially American is not American at all. The brass chandelier, the central stem of which is a series of globes from which emanate curved branches holding candle sockets, is an English import by way of Dutch inspiration. Most surviving examples of 18th-century brass chandeliers in America were in fact made in Bristol or in London. Such historic survivors became appreciated as "American" artifacts during the Colonial Revival of the late 19th century and have remained with us ever since as "Colonial" icons. That these brass chandeliers appear more formal than tin or wood and metal hanging fixtures may be partially explained by the fact that they were originally intended for churches. But this ecclesiastical function has long been eclipsed by the needs of the formal domestic interior.

1

2

3

4

5

6

7

Opposite page: **1.** The Taylor's Lane, a six-arm fixture by **William Spencer,** measures 22″ wide and 17″ high. The chandelier is crafted from blueprints used by the company since it was founded at the height of the Colonial Revival in 1897. **2.** The Lawrenceville, also by **William Spencer,** features six arms with glass globes. 22″ wide, 17″ high. **3.** Georgian grandeur is everywhere apparent in this fine replica by **Progress Lighting.** With eighteen electrified candles on two tiers, model TC-4388 is intended for a large room. 42″ wide, 32″ high. *This page:* **4.** A chandelier by **Price Glover Incorporated** is more than a superb reproduction. It is an antique of the future. Shown here is an exact reproduction of a boldly designed mid-18th-century English brass chandelier. The rare swirled gadrooning on the central ball repeats the detailing of the stem which is surmounted by a dove with outstretched wings. Also available wired. 35″ wide, 33½″ high. **5. Progress Lighting**'s model N1292, with twelve electrified arms on two tiers, is 36″ wide and 36″ high. **6. Price Glover**'s exact reproduction of a fine mid-18th-century brass chandelier is 30″ wide and 21″ high. **7.** The Saltbox's exquisite brass chandelier (PL-387-15), wiring optional, is 25″ wide and 24″ high.

1

5

2

3

4

1. Authentic Design's simple brass chandelier (CH-289) has three curving arms with crystal-clear globes. Electrified, it measures 10½″ wide and 16½″ high. It is also available in a 16″ width with six arms (CH-290).
2. Florence is a classic Federal hall fixture by **William Spencer**. It measures 12″ wide by 26″ high and has three lights and a 9″ smoke bell. William Spencer is an excellent source for several models of this hard-to-find foyer chandelier. **3-4.** Although **Hubbardton Forge & Wood Corporation** is primarily a custom forge where skilled craftsmen can forge metal to your specifications, it does stock many stand-

ard lighting designs. Shown here is a beautifully simple brass chandelier (#2105) equipped with and without Williamsburg globes.
5. Replicas of late-19th-century oil chandeliers are very difficult to locate, largely because owners of Victorian houses prefer ornamental gas fixtures. If you live in a country residence where gas lighting would have been a rarity, **Authentic Design**'s model CH-106 may be just right for you. 17″ wide, 17½″ high. *Opposite page:* **6. Price Glover**'s reproduction of an English hanging lantern is perfection itself. Also available electrified. 12″ wide, 28″ high.

Sconces

Few forms of early lighting are more simple—or more varied in design—than the sconce. With candles a scarce and valuable commodity in 18th-century North America, a way was needed to provide both a fixed place for a candleholder and a means to protect the candle from wax-wasting drafts. A primitive metal candleholder mounted on a wall removed from drafts was both functional and even decorative. Moreover, the metal often reflected candlelight, thereby increasing the illumination in a room. From the simple ornamentation of these first sconces developed more creative and elaborate designs. The variety of sconces crafted in the century before gaslight eventually eclipsed the candle is nothing short of astonishing, and the number of designs expertly reproduced by modern lighting artisans is an almost equal source of wonder and delight.

The range of inventive designs for early American wall fittings—from the simple to the ornate—can only be suggested in the pages that follow. In most cases, when electrified sconces are offered, the manufacturer assumes that the fixtures will be fitted to wall connections. Cords with switches can be requested, however, when wall connections are not possible.

1. The heart was a favorite Pennsylvania-German folk art motif, and **Authentic Design**'s heart-shaped sconce (SC2-210) would be suitably at home in any country-style room. The sconce is 13″ wide and 8½″ high. The arms extend 5″.

1

Shown here are four of **Authentic Design**'s most handsome wall fittings: **2.** The plate-shaped sconce (SC2-205) is 10″ wide and 10½″ high. The arms extend 5½″. **3.** Model SC1-139 is 4½″ wide and 9¾″ high. The looped arm extends 6¾″. **4.** Model SC2-228 reflects light in two different directions and extends from the wall at a pleasant angle. It measures 9″ wide, 12″ high, and 4½″ deep. **5.** The tulip-shaped sconce (SC1-121) is 7″ wide and 7½″ high. The arm extends 7″. **6.** Hurley **Patentee Lighting**'s dual-sided sconce is an exact replica of a Colonial innovation meant to spread precious candlelight to the sides. It is 10″ wide, 14″ high, and 5″ deep. **7.** **Hurley**'s candle-bearing brass sconce is 10″ wide, 12″ high, and 4″ deep.

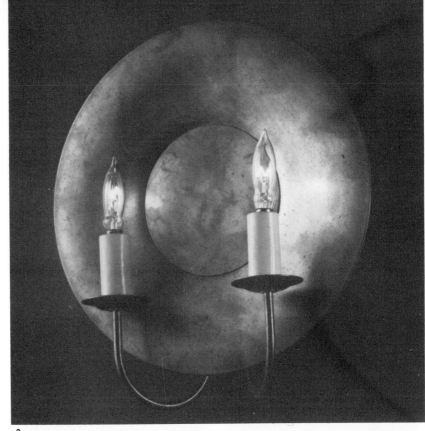

2

3

4

5

6

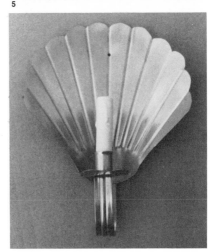

7

This page: **1.** Reproductions of primitive lighting acoutrements, all by **Lt. Moses Willard,** surround the Todd House sconce, which measures 5″ wide by 14″ high and is also available electrified. **2.** Among the many sconces made by **Gates Moore** in several finishes are the six models illustrated here. They range in height from 7″ to 12″. *Opposite page:* **3.** The Lined Holder, made by **Hurley Patentee Lighting,** measures 4½″ wide by 13½″ high. **4.** Handcrafted by the tinsmiths of **Hammerworks** and available in many different finishes is the electrified sconce (S 110), 8″ wide by 10″ high. **5.** Hammerworks' folk art sconce in a tulip motif (WI 102) is 6″ wide by 12″ high and is also available electrified. **6.** Hurley's Tin Crown sconce, an exact replica of a very early candleholder, measures 5″ wide by 18″ high. **7.** Hurley's Plain and Fancy brass sconce, only 5″ wide by 9″ high, is made in a pleasingly small size for both table and wall. **8.** Also by **Hurley** is this Flat-back sconce, 7″ wide by 12″ high, a primitive fixture with an unusually large reflector. **9.** Hammerworks' heart-shaped sconce (WI 107) holds two candles and measures 8½″ wide by 9″ high. **10.** Hurley's Tulip Top Holder is a tin sconce, 5″ wide by 14″ high, with a slightly rounded top. **11.** The Primitive Oval sconce, a very early tin candleholder reproduced by **Hurley,** is available with one, two, or three arms. The three-light sconce shown measures 12″ wide by 16″ high and projects 7″. **12.** Hurley's unusual hand-forged Iron Ring sconce, 11″ wide by 17″ high, comes complete with backplate and hook. **13.** Hammerworks' model S 112 is available in several finishes and is 4″ wide by 15″ high. All of the firm's electrified sconces are also made as candleholders. **14.** Hurley's Tall Corner sconce, 8″ wide by 18″ high, suggests the simple lines of Shaker design.

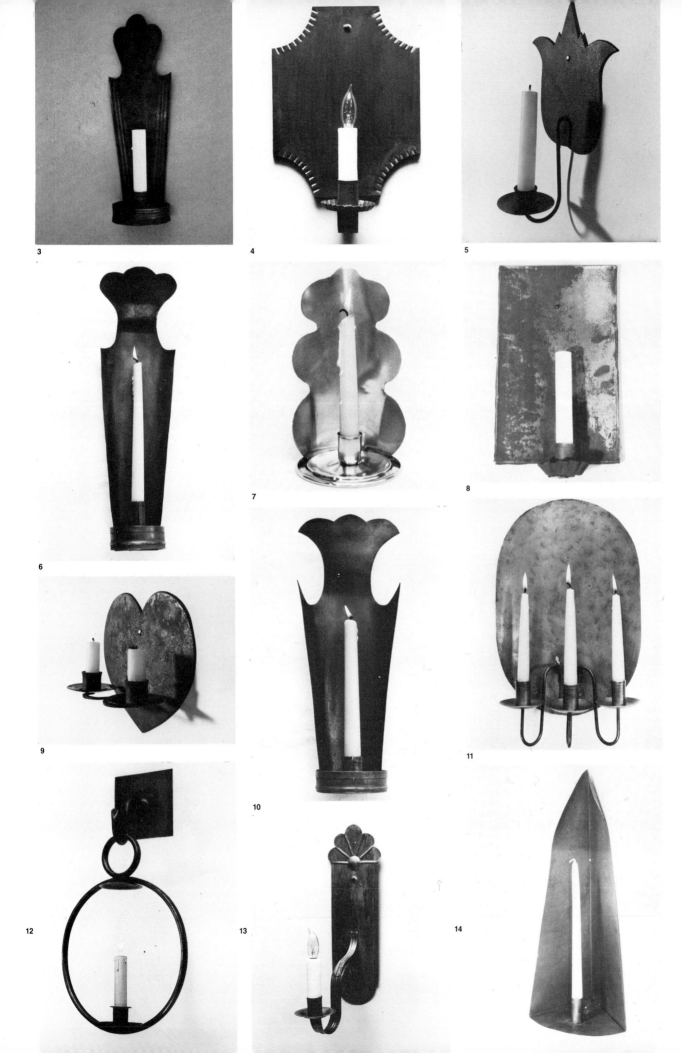

3

4

5

6

7

8

9

10

11

12

13

14

This page: **1.** Candlelight intensified by the many facets of a mirrored reflector once illuminated the rooms of the wealthy. This fine reproduction of a round mirrored sconce by **Period Furniture Hardware Co.** is 7″ wide and 10″ high and is available electrified or as a candleholder. **2.** A mirrored sconce with decorative crosshatching and a rounded piecrust top (S 106) is offered by **Hammerworks** and measures 5″ wide by 11″ high. **3.** Like other mirrored candleholders made by **Hurley Patentee Lighting,** the Diamond Mirror sconce features antiqued glass for greater authenticity. Measuring 5″ wide by 12″ high, the sconce, like almost all Hurley reproductions, is available electrified or fitted for candles. *Opposite page:* The sconces illustrated on this page, all by **Hurley Patentee Lighting,** illustrate not only the high standards of historical accuracy held to by this outstanding firm, but the originality of design conceived by our Colonial ancestors. The Hurley sconces that follow are astonishing in their versatility. **4.** The Pennsylvania Mirror sconce, 4″ wide by 13″ high, employs the heart motif favored by the early Pennsylvania Germans. **5.** The Oval Mirror sconce, 9″ wide by 16″ high, reflects the very essence of Colonial simplicity. **6.** This larger version of Hurley's Diamond Mirror sconce measures 10″ wide by 17″ high. **7.** Just as modern make-up mirrors are illuminated, Colonial looking glasses were sometimes candle-lit. This handsome looking glass sconce, 12″ wide by 20″ high, is made of tin decorated at the edges. The gracefully curved candleholders project 8½″. **8.** The Cabriole Look-

1

2

3

4

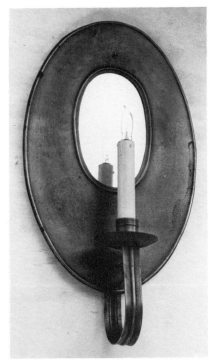

5

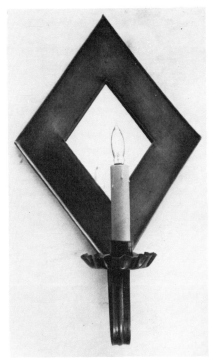

6

7

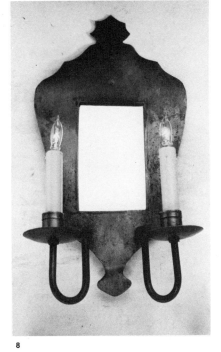

8

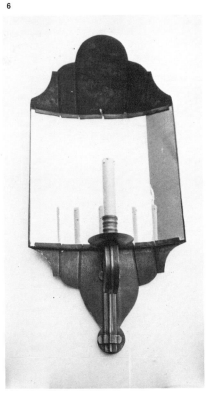

9

ing Glass sconce, with its attractively shaped tin backplate, measures 7½″ wide by 17″ high. **9.** The five-sided mirror of the Majestic Mirror sconce creates the illusion of many lights with the reflections of a single candle. The large tin sconce, 11½″ wide by 25″ high, projects 7½″.

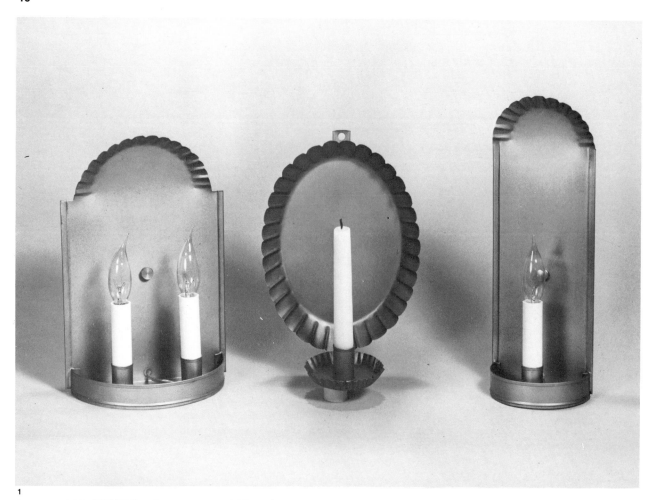

1

2

3

4

Opposite page: **1.** Renowned today for their simple and practical designs, the pietistic Shakers of the last century anticipated the functional lines of modernism by many, many decades. As its name indicates, **Shaker Workshops** excels in the reproduction of 19th-century Shaker artifacts, including the three antiqued tin sconces illustrated here. All three, reflecting the Shakers' almost timeless sense of design, are available electrified or as candleholders. They measure, left to right, 7″ wide by 11″ high, 8″ wide by 11″ high, and 4½″ wide by 12″ high. **2.** The tin Perched Eagle sconce by **Hurley Patentee Lighting** takes its name from its interestingly shaped backplate. Measuring 9″ wide and 17″ high, the sconce is also available with three candleholders in both electrified and non-electrified models. **3.** Alternating long and short lines decorate **Hurley**'s Lined Plate sconce, an early sconce with a slight forward rounding. It is 10″ wide, 13″ high, and 5″ deep. **4. Hurley**'s two-light Arch Sconce takes its name from the primitive design on the backplate. It is 9″ wide, 14″ high and 5″ deep. Like most Hurley sconces, it comes either electrified or non-electrified. *This page:* **5. Hammerworks**' model S 120 features a piecrust top and a backplate pierced in a double-heart design. Handmade in either antiqued tin or antiqued brass and copper, the sconce measures 7″ wide and 13¾″ high and is also available in a candle-bearing model. **6.** Dusk and the need for artificial light combine symbolically in the handsome Sunset Sconce handcrafted in tin by **Hurley Patentee Lighting**. The three-light wall fixture measures 18″ wide, 12″ high, and 4″ deep and is also available wired.

1

2

One of the most frequently encountered decorative motifs of early tinwork, and one very often employed in the making of sconces, is the crimped piecrust design. Used either entirely surrounding the fixture, including the drip pan, or as only one element in an overall design, the piecrust motif, like other early decorative devices, appears over and over again in pleasing configurations of almost endless versatility. *This page:* **1.** This platter-shaped three-candle sconce (S 102) by **Hammerworks** is wider than it is tall. Like other handmade sconces from this maker of antique reproductions, it is also available electrified and in several finishes, and measures 11″ wide by 6⅜″ high. **2.** Employing the piecrust design at the top and bottom of the backplate and also around the drip pan, **Lt. Moses Willard**'s model 2160, like all the firm's sconces, comes in a variety of finishes. Measuring 4½″ wide by 3½″ high, the sconce is also available electrified. *Opposite page:* **3.** With the top of its backplate and its drip pans simply crimped, **Hammerworks**' model S 115B is also available in a single-arm model (S 115A). Both are 3½″ wide by 9¾″ high. **4.** **Hurley Patentee Lighting**'s tin Bonnet Top holder may be used on a table or on a wall. Available unelectrified as well, it measures 3″ wide by 9″ high. **5.** **Hurley**'s delightful Heart Sconce (SC 337) features crossing candleholders that project from the base of the folk art backplate. The sconce can also be ordered fully wired. **6.** Combining the piecrust motif with punchwork tulips, **Hammerworks**' model S 118 is pleasingly proportioned at 7¼″ wide by 12½″ high. **7, 8.** Also by **Hammerworks** are models S 113 and S 101, respectively. The former measures 6″ wide and 11″ high; the

3

4

5

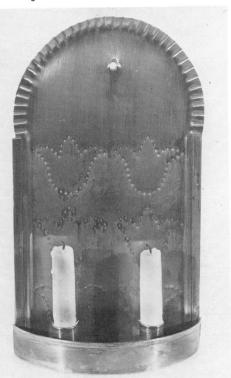

6

7

8

latter comes in two sizes—3⅜″ wide by 14¼″ high and 4½″ wide by 14¼″ high. All Hammerworks sconces are available wired or with candle sockets and are finished in antique tin, rust, milk paint (red, brown, blue, or black), copper, brass, or iron.

3

2

4

While rather closely restricted in general form, tin sconces delight the eye with an infinite variety of detail which, now and again, expands into delightful fantasy. Although **Hurley Patentee Lighting**'s collection of reproduction wall fittings includes almost every type of Colonial sconce, its selection of fancifully designed sconces is unexcelled. The seven Hurley sconces shown here and on the opposite page can only suggest the artistry of our forebears, now faithfully reproduced for our own period rooms. *Opposite page:* **1.** The Diamond Disc sconce is a rare reflector fixture of Colonial elegance and is made of wood and tin with a glass front. The encased discs and backplate are made of antique leaded tin, giving them the look of pewter. The fixture measures 10½″ wide, 15″ high, and 5″ deep. **2.** The tin Sunflower Sconce is 9½″ wide by 12″ high. The candleholder extends 5″. **3.** The Iron Ring Disc sconce is another rare reflecting fixture and measures 11″ wide, 12½″ high, and 5″ deep. The discs and the backplate are of antique leaded tin. **4.** The Shield and Leaf sconce features a punch-work tulip design and measures 9″ wide, 13½″ high, and 6″ deep. *This page:* **5.** The Pineapple Sconce is in every way true to the lines of its tropical namesake. Of probable Pennsylvania origin, it measures 7″ wide, 15″ high, and 3″ deep. **6.** The Raised Reflector sconce, an unusual two-light fixture with humped center reflector and crimped drip plate, is made of tin and measures 8″ wide, 10″ high, and 3″ deep. **7.** The Fluted Arch sconce is a brass fixture with a punchwork and embossed backplate. It is 6½″ wide, 11″ high, and 3″ deep. Note that all Hurley sconces are available in electrified and non-electrified models.

5

6

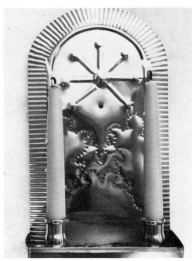

7

1

2

3

Period sconces with 20th-century lampshades may bemuse historical purists, but no one can deny their peculiar charms. Particularly at home in a country setting, such pin-up lamps have many uses.
1. The Iron Strap Lamp by **The Essex Forge** is functionally attractive and fits well into most decorative schemes. Equipped with an 8″ oyster-white burlap shade, the lamp is 18″ long with a 7″ arm and a 72″ plug-in cord. **2. Hurley Patentee Lighting**'s Shade and Bracket sconce is made of iron and tin and is available electrified or non-electrified (the shade is made of tin). It measures 7″ wide by 12″ high, and the arm extends 9½″.
3. Lt. Moses Willard's plug-in pin-up lamp (model 2170) is available with or without the pierced-tin shade. It is 4½″ wide by 13½″ high.

Like brass chandeliers, brass sconces in the English manner are suitable for formal rooms. Surprisingly, good reproductions of

5

4

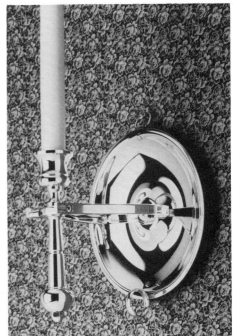

6

formal brass sconces are very difficult to come by, though the three fixtures on this page should go a long way towards satisfying even the most finicky tastes. **4. Price Glover Incorporated** imports precise reproductions of antique English brass wall sconces in one-, two-, and three-arm models, each with tulip-

shaped shades in clear or green crystal. The sconces are also available with crystal bobeches with drops and come either electrified or non-electrified. The triple sconce shown measures 18″ wide, 22″ high, and 9″ deep. **5.** Like its other reproductions of fine English fixtures, **Price Glover**'s candle sconce

is a work of art unto itself. Cast by the lost wax process, it is entirely hand finished. **6.** The Gimbal Chamberstick was originally used on ships to keep the candle level on a rolling sea. **Baldwin Giftware**'s reproduction can be used as a sconce (as shown) or, base down, as a tabletop candleholder.

Lanterns

The lantern is the most versatile of lighting devices. It can be carried, hung, affixed to almost any surface, or simply left standing on a table or shelf. Most lanterns are enclosed on all sides as they were originally designed for use indoors and out, crafted to burn effectively under the most adverse conditions. All, however, are vented in some manner and are built with one panel that can be opened for changing the light source. Although in use for many centuries, the lantern was not common in the North American colonies until the late 18th century. Thanks to Longfellow's romanticized notions of Paul Revere, the lantern is still viewed as the quintessential "Colonial" lighting device. Reproduction lanterns of all sizes, shapes, and forms are available today. Most of them are terrible. On the pages that follow are the exceptions to this unfortunate rule—lanterns that are sturdily constructed and offer solid value for each dollar spent.

1. In the belief, shared by us, that the natural aging of copper enhances the beauty of lanterns, all **Lt. Moses Willard** lanterns are handcrafted of solid copper and are antiqued to resemble naturally aged copper. Shown clockwise from the far right are #5020, with glass on all four sides to make it suitable for hanging (7″ wide, 13½″ high, 7″ deep); #5120, a wall-mounted lantern with glass on three sides (8″ by 16½″ by 6½″); #5130, a hanging lantern (7″ by 16″ by 7″); #5140, a wall-mounted lantern (5″ by 16½″ by 5″); #5010, a hanging lantern (9″ by 18″ by 9″); #5110, a wall-mounted lantern with one pane of sliding glass and pierced sides (6″ by 10½″ by 4″); and #5060, a wall-mounted lantern (7½″ by 14½″ by 7″). Lt. Moses Willard lanterns can be protected with clear lacquer or painted flat black upon request. They are available with either clear glass or seedy acrylic panels.

1

2

3

6

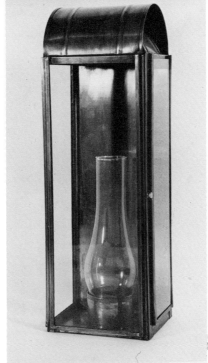

4

7

5

2. Hurley Patentee Lighting's Wood and Pierced Tin lantern is a reproduction of one of the earliest Colonial hanging lanterns. It measures 6½" wide, 10" high, and 5½" deep. A slightly larger version with back reflector is available for wall mounting. **3.** The Higganum lantern by **The Essex Forge** is a replica of an 18th-century barn lamp. It is 6¾" wide, 16" high, and 7½" deep and is also available wall-mounted.

4. Hammerworks' Tall Ship model, a traditional ship's lantern meant for wall mounting, is available in copper or brass and measures 7½" wide, 21" high, and 6" deep. **5. The Washington Copper Works'** model KL1-S is a kerosene-burning lantern that can be carried about because the handle stays cool. It will not blow out in any wind and measures 7" wide, 27" high, and 7" deep.

6. The copper or brass barn lantern by **Hammerworks**, adapted for wall mounting, is available in two sizes: 8" by 17½" by 8½" and 10" by 21" by 8½". **7. The Washington Copper Works'** oil lamp sconce comes electrified (as shown) or with an oil burner and measures 5¾" wide, 17" high, and 5¾" deep.

1

2

3

4

5

6

1. Liz's Lantern, designed and crafted by **The Washington Copper Works**, is a large, bold fixture for the front entryway and is available as a two-light oil lamp or electrified. In the latter model, socket adapters enable the user to illuminate with small 7½-watt candelabra bulbs or any standard-base bulb up to 60-watts. The fixture is 12″ wide, 24″ high, and 7″ deep. **2.** The Chapin, an adaptation of the Colonial lantern for modern homes by **The Washington Copper Works**, features a glass bottom for dramatic downlighting. It measures 7″ wide, 19½″ high, and 7″ deep. **3.** American Period Lighting Fixtures by **The Saltbox** offers a large number of period lanterns reproduced from originals in historic collections. One of the most popular is Model PL 1033, a brass fixture 10½″ wide, 28″ high, and 9½″ deep. It is also available in smaller sizes by request. **4.** Mill House lanterns, crafted by **The Washington Copper Works**, come in many sizes. All but the smallest, pictured here, are designed for outdoor use and include rain guards over the doors, bug-screens to keep the fixture insect-free, and conduit tubes to cover the wires. The largest Mill House lantern is 19½″ high; the smallest, just 12″ high, is proportioned for indoor use. **5.** **The Washington Copper Works**' Hexagonal Candle Lantern, though not wall-mounted, is a conversation piece and an exercise in optical illusion. With see-through mirrors used for the three rear panes and distressed, antiqued glass used for the front three, the lantern is simultaneously reflective and transparent. Measuring 6¾″ wide, 13″ high, and 9″ deep, the lantern comes equipped with a candle snuffer. **6.** **The Saltbox**'s wall-mounted lantern, L77, with Colonial-style reflector, is 7½″ wide and 22″ high.

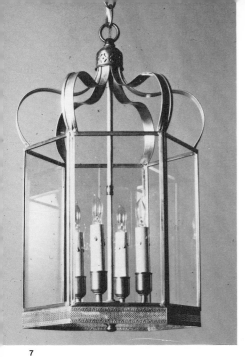

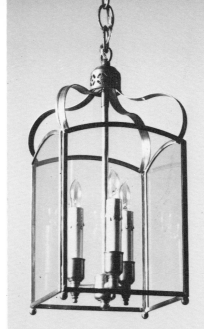

7

8

9

10

11

12

Lanterns were originally versatile fixtures. They were designed to be carried for outdoor use and hung for indoor illumination, particularly in the front hall near a staircase. This multiple use explains why today's suppliers, bowing to the requirements of fixed electrical installations, will frequently offer the same lantern design in wall, table, and hanging models. The hanging lanterns illustrated here barely suggest the variety offered to today's consumers. **7,8.** The English Hall Light, a brass fixture by **The Saltbox** and shown here at two different angles, is available in four different sizes. **9.** One of **Newstamp Lighting**'s Deerfield series, lanterns handcrafted from copper and brass and available in several finishes, is this distinctly modern adaptation of the lantern form. Featuring downlights integrated into the design of the fixture—an impossibility before electric light—the lantern is available in two sizes, the smaller of which is half the double lantern shown here. **10.** Though equally appealing, **Hurley Patentee Lighting**'s Hexagonal Hall Lantern is closer to historical reality. Available electrified or fitted for candles, the fixture is 8″ wide and 17″ high. **11.** Onion Globe lanterns, once very popular, are difficult to find today. **Newstamp Lighting**'s New Bedford series includes a variety of these nautical lanterns for every need, from ceiling to post. Shown here is one of several hanging models. **12. Newstamp**'s Marblehead series captures the straightforwardness of Colonial design in a line of lanterns for post, wall, and ceiling mount. The hanging lantern shown is available in a number of sizes and in a number of bulb configurations.

1

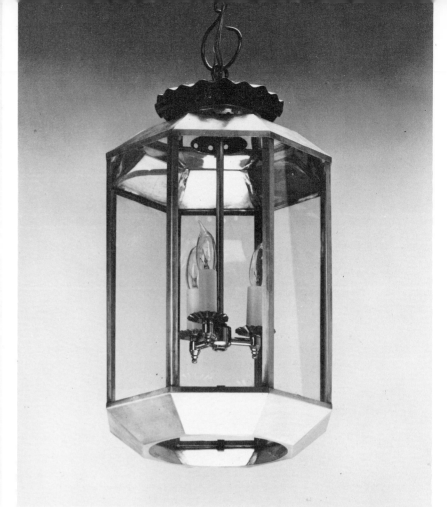

2

3

4

5

6

8

9

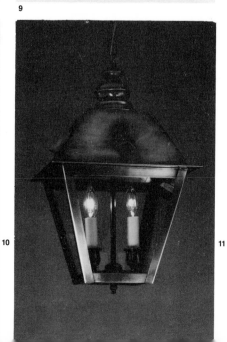

10

11

Opposite page: **1.** Wendy's Light by **The Washington Copper Works** is a basic hexagonal hall lantern, unadorned and handsome. Available with a three-light cluster as shown, or in a smaller version with two lights, the fixture measures 8½″ wide by 12″ high. **2.** A variation on the same theme is **Washington Copper Works'** octagonal hanging light. Available in a standard size of 12″ wide by 18″ high, the fixture can also be made to your own specifications. **3.** The same firm produces this simple hexagonal lantern, decorated with either horizontal guards, as shown, or with spiral guards that encircle the fixture in two bands. The lanterns are available in six sizes, from 8″ wide and 13″ high to 16″ wide and 20″ high. **4.** The faint French Provincial styling of **Newstamp Lighting**'s solid-brass hall fixture makes it suitable for traditional rather than period interiors. It is available in three- or four-light models. **5.** **Newstamp**'s Beacon Hill lanterns come in post, wall, and hanging models. The fixture shown is available in three sizes, the largest of which is 13″ wide and 24″ high. **6.** The small size of **Washington Copper Works'** Gunnery (7″ wide, 10″ high) makes it ideal for small halls and even bathrooms. **7.** This no-nonsense, classic ceiling light by **Gates Moore** (10 B) measures 6″ by 14″ or 8″ by 16½″. It can be ordered without canopy and metal top to fit flush with the ceiling. **8.** Wendy's Light decorated with spiral guards (see **1**). **9. Hurley Patentee Lighting**'s historically accurate wood and glass lantern is available in sizes that accommodate from one to three lights, electrified or non-electrified. **10.** The hanging version of the Higganum lantern by **The Essex Forge** measures 6¾″ wide and 16″ high. **11. Newstamp Lighting**'s 82 HC estate lantern comes in three sizes. The two-light model shown is 10½″ wide and 18″ high.

1

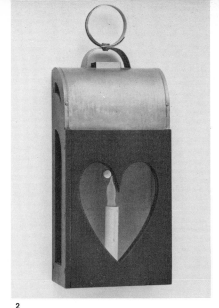

2

3

4

5

6

7

Opposite page: **1.** Although tradition tells us that Paul Revere's legendary lantern was a tin punchwork affair, no pierced-tin lantern could possibly have cast sufficient light to warn the rebel Colonists that the British were coming. Still, the legend persists. **Lt. Moses Willard** offers its version of the Revere lantern—electrified and pierced in a sunburst pattern. Seen with the 7″-wide, 16½″-high lantern is a miniature four-light hall fixture, just 8″ wide and 12½″ high. *This page:* **2.** A fanciful heart lantern, available as a wall sconce as shown or as a freestanding lantern, is offered by **Lt. Moses Willard**. At 6½″ wide by 19″ high, it may not have history behind it, but it certainly has charm. **3.** Copper lanterns from **Gates Moore** can be oxidized or painted to simulate age. Model 20, shown, has a mirror reflector and measures 9″ wide, 17″ high, and 9″ deep. A larger size is also available. **4.** The handsome Essex lantern by **The Essex Forge** is made of copper and measures 10″ wide, 21″ high, and 8½″ deep. It can be finished in antique black if so desired. **5.** Reproduced from the original at the Griswold Inn in Essex, Connecticut, the solid-copper Griswold lantern by **The Essex Forge** features a crimped reflector and is 5″ wide, 13″ high, and 6¾″ deep. **6.** The 605B lantern, available in several finishes, is part of **Newstamp Lighting**'s Marblehead series. Measuring 10″ wide, 26″ high, and 4¾″ deep, it is also offered in a smaller size. **7.** It's traditional, ubiquitous, and safe, but the Baltimore Coach Lamp by **Newstamp Lighting** is also a design classic. Redolent of the days of horseless carriages, the brass fixture is offered in two sizes (18″ or 25″ high).

1

2

3

4

5

6

7

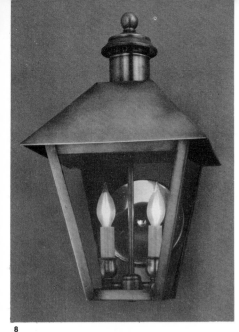

8

9

10

11

12

13

Opposite page: **1.** Designed to fit snugly in a corner, the handsome and practical Tricon lantern by **Hammerworks** is available in either brass or copper finishes and measures 13″ wide, 17½″ high, and 10½″ deep. **2.** Unlike most lanterns, **Newstamp Lighting**'s model 610B accents the horizontal rather than the vertical. Made of copper and brass, it measures 15½″ wide, 17″ high, and 6″ deep. **3.** Once found on every second bungalow between Long Island City and Oakland, California, this simple porch lantern, well crafted by **Hammerworks**, deserves its renewed popularity today. Available in copper or brass, it comes in three different sizes, the smallest of which is 7″ wide, 14″ high, and 7″ deep. **4,5.** Metalworker Ned James of **Mill River Hammerworks** will custom-design and craft the ideal lantern to suit your individual needs. The two lanterns shown illustrate how graceful form, subtle detail, and careful execution mark his work. **6.** If you prefer a lantern above your door rather than a pair at the sides, then **Newstamp Lighting**'s 507B-SA is the choice for you. The fixture's span is 32″. **7.** The solid-copper Downey lantern by **Lt. Moses Willard** boasts a brass reflector plate and measures 9⅜″ wide, 18″ high, and 5⅞″ deep. *This page:* **8.** Made of copper and brass, **Newstamp Lighting**'s 3BC lantern is 11″ wide, 18″ high, and 11½″ deep. A smaller size is also available. **9.** The Auburn, a ship's lantern by **Hammerworks**, is available in copper and brass and measures 10″ wide, 27½″ high, and 7½″ deep. **10.** The Salem series of solid-brass lanterns by **Newstamp Lighting** suggests the clipper ship era in that New England port. **11.** One of many onion dome lanterns made by **Newstamp**. **12.** The Gunnery wall light by **The Washington Copper Works** is 7″ wide, 14½″ high, and 7″ deep. **13.** For use on a table or a wall, **Hurley Patentee Lighting**'s lantern sconce is multifunctional and handsome. It is 6″ wide, 13″ high, and 4″ deep and is also made in a candle-socket model.

1. The lantern hasn't been devised yet that Serge Miller can't build in the workshop of his **Washington Copper Works.** His work is very personal. Even lanterns based on Colonial models emerge from the bench with a look that defines it as an original work and not merely a reproduction. Miller has an uncanny talent for adapting an ancient form and re-creating it for the contemporary home. As several lanterns illustrated on this page and the page opposite attest, Miller's Colonial-inspired lanterns can be very modern indeed. **2.** The Burnham is named for the man who first created the handsome bracket hook that holds the lantern. The fixture measures 5¼″ wide, 19½″ high, and 6″ deep. **3.** The Rumsey is a stately updating of the lantern form. At 9″ wide, 23″ high, and 6″ deep, it has a glass bottom for subtle downlighting. **4.** The HLS hexagonal lantern features spiral guards and is available in six different sizes. **5.** The Houston C is a modern lantern with glass bottom and comes in two sizes: 7″ wide, 12″ high, and 4½″ deep; and 5″ by 9″ by 4″. **6.** The San Giuliano lantern is designed hexagonally for both indoor use and out and is made in three sizes, ranging in height from 12″ to 15″. **7.** The Houston D is a variation of the Houston C and measures 9″ wide, 18″ high, and 6″ deep. All lanterns by The Washington Copper Works are initialed and dated.

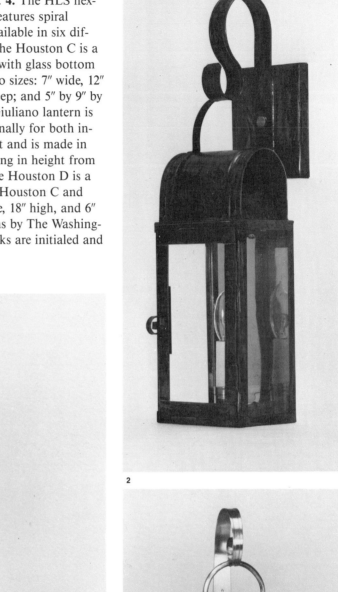

2

1

3

4

5

6

7

67

Post Lanterns

Among the ugliest of modern objects to be seen along our streets and roads today are lighting standards. They often appear to stand as alien creatures, and even neighborhood dogs are reluctant to pause beneath their ungainly shapes. Yet, as many homeowners have discovered in rural and suburban areas, outdoor fixtures needn't be so unattractive and forbidding. Graceful standards are available for both municipal and home lighting, and these are capped with similarly handsome lanterns, worlds apart from the horrors found in suburban home centers. Outdoor gas lighting (see Welsbach Lighting in List of Suppliers) has returned to use in some urban historic districts, and the proper types of fixtures, ubiquitous in the 19th century, are being made once again.

Opposite page: **1.** Tracing its origins to an iron foundry begun in 1843, **Spring City Electrical Manufacturing Company** is the prime producer of ornamental lighting posts in North America. Several of its many light standards are suitable for domestic properties, including the Franklin Post, the earliest (c. 1751) post style in the New World. It is available in variable heights from 8'9½" to 12' (excluding lantern). *This page:* **2.** The Sudbury, by **Newstamp Lighting**, is a post lantern that is 10½" wide and 27" high with a 3" post collar. Made also in a smaller size, it is available in brass, copper, or black finishes. **3.** The Boston Street Light by **Hammerworks** is a classic lantern measuring 15½" wide by 43" high (also 13" wide by 38" high). **4.** Also by **Hammerworks** is the Wills Post Lantern, 16½" wide by 39" high. All Hammerworks lanterns are made of either copper or brass.

2

3

4

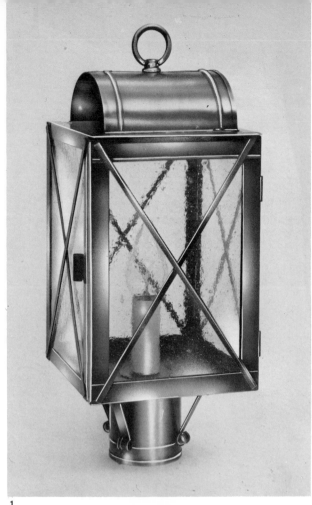

1

2

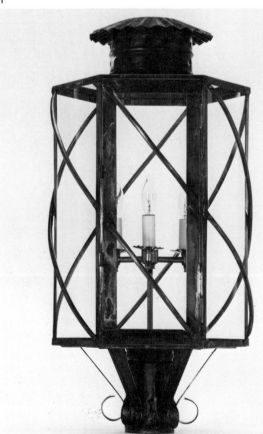

3

4

Besides lighting the way to the door, post lights provide a cheerful welcome to the night visitor. While self-consciously cute if designed by hands less practiced than the manufacturers represented here, post lights are in every way preferable to the floodlit look of Alcatraz, increasingly popular in these security-conscious days. *Opposite page:* **1.** The traditional lines of **Newstamp Lighting**'s model 58P post lantern are complemented by antique seedy glass panels. The lantern is 7½″ wide and 18″ high with a 3″ post collar. **2.** The Garrison, by **Hammerworks**, is made in two sizes—11″ wide by 26″ high and 9½″ by 21″—and available in either copper or brass. **3.** The Exeter post light, by **The Washington Copper Works**, is made in various design configurations. Model PL53L features spiral guards and a three-light cluster and comes in two sizes— 13½″ wide by 26″ high and 11″ by 22½″. **4.** The Coach Lantern, by **Hammerworks**, is another variation on the Colonial theme and measures 18″ wide by 31″ high. *This page:* **5.** While the revolutionary troops at Lexington might not recognize it as of their time, **The Washington Copper Works**' Lexington is not without considerable fictive charm. It is 12″ wide and 35″ high. **6. Newstamp Lighting**'s Beacon Hill estate lantern echoes the splender of 19th-century Boston's cobblestone streets. It is available in two sizes—15″ wide by 42″ high and 13″ by 31″, both with 3″ post collars. **7. Spring City Electrical Manufacturing Company**'s Independence Post, is an iron replica of a Colonial lighting post authenticated by researchers at Philadelphia's Independence National Historic Park. Its octagonal base measures 5½″; the height of the post is 7′3″, excluding the luminaire. **8.** The Edgartown, a post lantern in copper or brass by **Hammerworks**, is 15″ wide and 36″ high.

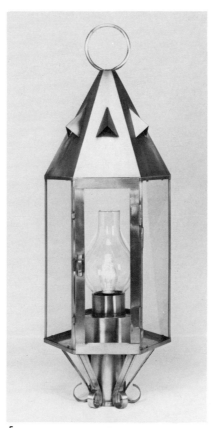

5

6

7

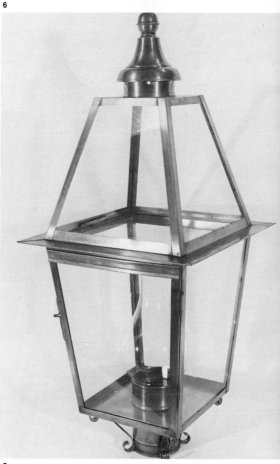

8

2   3

Gasoliers

The gradual acceptance of gaslight as the most progressive mode of 19th-century illumination made possible the general lighting of domestic interiors. Before the Victorian period, candleholders and the first oil lamps provided concentrated light for small areas of a room, but overhead lighting was a rarity limited to public buildings and the houses of the very rich. An almost immediate result of the widespread use of hanging gasoliers was a freer arrangement of household furniture. With antique fixtures still available, if expensive, and with reproductions made by an increasing number of contemporary firms, the best of which are represented in these pages, no Victorian parlor or dining room can afford to be without an electrified gasolier. As light is reflected from its polished metallic surfaces and filtered through its colorful etched shades, a well-wrought reproduction gasolier can become the dramatic centerpiece of such period rooms.

As a general rule, gas fixtures of the early Victorian period, when gaslight was far more rare and expensive than it became at the end of the century, are much more ornate and elaborately designed than later gasoliers. Early gas chandeliers are also recognizable because of their round glass globes, typical of gasolier shades before wide-based shades were introduced in 1876. **1.** Typical of early gasoliers built on the grand scale is **Progress Lighting**'s Classical Revival gasolier (TC 4048), a reproduction of a documented original made by Cornelius and Co. in the 1840s and authenticated by Roger Moss, executive director of the Athenaeum of Philadelphia. The brass and crystal gasolier measures 29″ in diameter and 32″ in height. With gaspipe stem, the overall length ranges from 35″ to 48″. A matching sconce is also available. **2. Classic Illumination**'s model 1880 is a solid-brass reproduction of a gasolier of the 1880s and is available with from two to six arms. The fixture has a spread of 30″ and a variable height of from 26″ to 62″, depending on length of gaspipe. A matching sconce and a variety of shades are offered. **3.** Also from **Classic Illumination** is the Griffin gasolier, a reproduction of a period fixture from c. 1870. Available with from two to six arms and with a choice of shades, the gasolier is crafted of solid brass and has a 30″ spread. A matching sconce is also offered.

1, 2, 3. **Roy Electric Company**, which features one of the largest selections of Victorian lighting reproductions in North America, has a first-hand knowledge of period lighting. As electrical contractors for over twenty years, the firm rewired, restored, and refurbished lighting fixtures in vintage New York brownstones and town houses, collecting and studying rare fixtures in an effort to discover how best to reproduce them with care and historical accuracy. Using solid brass, Roy Electric combines 19th-century hand-craftsmanship with modern technology to produce Victorian pieces that are as handsome, but far safer, than their 19th-century prototypes. The firm's brass artisans are very versatile and can make any of the gasoliers shown here in larger or smaller sizes. All fixtures can also be crafted using different styles of brass tubing, including rope, reeded, or plain. Shown on this page from top left are Roy's models GS 12-6, GS 10-4, and GS 5-3. 4, 5. **Roy Electric**'s model GS 13-9 is adorned with elaborate brass scrollwork. In contrast, the twin-armed model GS 7-2 is virtually unadorned. 6. The craftsmen at **Victorian Reproductions** have also put the experience gained repairing antique fixtures to good use in producing expert reproductions such as their model 2500-6, a six-arm gasolier. 7, 8. Like all of its fixtures, **Roy Electric**'s models GS 9-2 (left) and GS 4-3 can be ordered with any number of arms to suit customer specifications. 9. Model 8600-1 from **Victorian Reproductions** would be a good choice for an entrance hall. 10. **Roy Electric**'s model GS 6-4 is shown here with graceful bowl-shaped shades. 11. **Victorian Reproductions** makes its model 8300-1 available through **Crawford's Old House Store** or direct from its Minneapolis office.

1. Victorian Lightcrafters has been restoring and selling antique lighting fixtures since 1971. Original Victorian fixtures are not in plentiful enough supply to satisfy the rapidly increasing demand, however, so the company introduced a line of quality reproductions in 1979. All are made of solid brass, soldered and assembled by hand. They can be polished and lacquered upon request. The firm's model C-1000 is a six-arm gas chandelier, 41″ wide, which can be ordered in lengths ranging from 36″ to 55″ according to ceiling height. Shown with etched-glass, amber-rimmed shades, the fixture can be fitted with a choice of other styles depending upon individual preference.

1

2

While any one of the superbly crafted reproductions shown on this page could be just what you're looking for to accent a particular wall or hallway, bear in mind that such a period piece is designed, as were the originals, to be used in fairly spacious surroundings. Most of these gas sconces extend at least a foot from the wall; carelessly placed at head height or below, they could easily be broken in a confined, heavily trafficked space.

2. Victorian Lightcrafters' model W651 is featured here with a clear pressed-glass shade. Its dimensions are 7″ by 9″; extension is 14″.

3

4

3. M-H Lamp & Fan Company began, as do so many period lighting firms, by restoring antique fixtures. Today the major part of its business is in the manufacture of reproductions such as this one (model 8330). Fitted with an amber satin-glass shade in a floral pattern, it extends 14½″ from the wall. Many other styles of shade may be substituted according to individual preference. **4. Roy Electric** is best known for its period chandeliers, but its sconces are no less expert in design and execution. Model S-G1 is a simply crafted single-arm fixture, shown here with a clear pressed-glass shade. **5. Classic Illumination** is well known in the field of restoration lighting; the firm has consulted on many restoration projects across the country, and its expertise assures the authenticity of its Victorian reproductions, including model 1875-1, pictured here. The mythical griffin is portrayed in brass on the arm of this elaborate sconce; its lion's head holds a delicately etched patterned shade. **6, 7. Victorian Lightcrafters'** model W205 is fitted with a clear glass engraved shade decorated with two frosted bands. The twin-armed model W310-D has etched satin-glass shades.

5

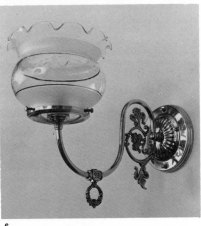

6

7

Gas and Electric Fixtures

In the early 1890s, the Fixture & Decorative Bronze Department of the Edison General Electric Co., the forerunner of today's GE, advertised "the latest in electric lights and combination gas fixtures." What the company meant by "combination gas fixtures" were lighting devices that burned gas and also had electrical elements. With electrical service, in the areas that had it, not exactly reliable, and with service limited to only certain hours of the day, the Edison Company was not hedging its bets. Until service improved, users of electric lights would rely, at least part of the time, on the ubiquity of gas. Transitional lighting fixtures are delightful devices in which gas burners always face ceilingwards while incandescent bulbs point downwards. They are frequently reproduced today and are suitable for turn-of-the-century interiors.

1. Since 1954, **Nowell's** has grown into one of the nation's most respected makers of Victorian lighting reproductions. Each fixture is made by hand in exactly the way the originals were constructed. The Pacific Club model illustrated is a six-arm gas and electric ballroom chandelier which measures 36″ wide and from 36″ to 42″ high. The unusual snowflake shades are of etched crystal, made from the original molds. **2.** This enormous ballroom chandelier (GES 8-12) would obviously be a suitable choice for only the most stately of Victorian mansions, if not public buildings and large restaurants. **Roy Electric**, experts at supplying lighting for large spaces, can reproduce it in widths from 38″ to 60″ and in heights of 15 feet or

1

2

3

more. (While such elaborate fixtures are the pride and joy of Roy and Roz Greenstein, proprietors of Roy Electric, they also offer equally handsome reproductions for more humble rooms, several of which are shown on the following pages.

3. Progress Lighting's model TC 4067 is a faithful reproduction of a design first made by Gibson Fixture Works around 1900. The polished brass arms have bead and melon decorations; the gas cocks are embellished with cast ribbon designs. The lovely shades are opalescent hand-blown glass; the swirled pattern ends in graceful hand-ruffled edges.

1. Crawford's Old House Store
retails selected lighting fixtures
crafted by the best American
manufacturers. For that reason,
you'll find this three-light combination gas and electric fixture in both
Crawford's catalogue and in that of
Victorian Reproductions (model
8100-3). Only 14″ wide, it is fitted
with frosted cut-glass shades.
2. The craftsmen at **The Classic Illumination** are specialists in custom
design and restoration. In addition,
however, the company offers a line
of 19th-century-inspired fixtures,
some much more elaborate than the
graceful two-light hanging lamp illustrated. A reproduction of a late
19th-century original, model 1890-1
is primarily intended for an entryway, hall, or kitchen. It can be
ordered in lengths ranging from 26″
to 62″, and is fitted with etched
glass shades. **3.** If you equate good
design with symmetry, you'll appreciate this balanced combination
fixture from **Victorian Reproductions** (also available from **Crawford's Old House Store**). Its twin
electric arms flank the central gas
shade; all three lights are fitted with
satin-etched shades of amber glass.
Even the ruffled edges of the
shades seem to mimic the curves of
the rope brass tubing. **4.** The delicate cut-glass shades and graceful
arms of this lovely fixture make it
suitable for the most romantic of
interiors. **M-H Lamp & Fan Company**'s model 8338 is embellished
with rope brass accents. **5. Roy
Electric**'s model GES 1-4 is small
enough to be just the right accent
in a modestly proportioned hallway
or dining room. Only 20″ wide, it is
adjustable to heights of between 24″
and 30″ and, like all the company's
fixtures, can be ordered with any

1

2

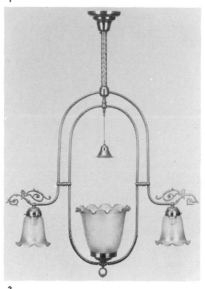

3

4

5

6

7

8

number of arms to suit individual requirements. **6, 7.** Because **Roy Electric** is located in Brooklyn, home of many superbly maintained turn-of-the-century brownstones, its craftsmen have no lack of inspiration and example for the authentic reproduction chandeliers they produce. These are two such examples (GES 7-6 and GES 5-8), both fashioned of the finest brass, and equally well suited for the most elegant Victorian surroundings. **8.** Gas or electric standards mounted on newel posts were far more common in the Victorian period than one might expect. Conditioned as we are by Hollywood's evocation of the age of gaslight, we associate the illuminated newel post with the mansions of the Robber Barons and their social set. Although the well-to-do most certainly installed some sumptuously ornamented examples in their villas and estates, the middle classes could choose from hundreds of more modest styles listed in the catalogues of such lighting manufacturers as Philadelphia's Cornelius & Sons. In addition, the bronze statues of knights and cavaliers and other figures that were so popular in the late 19th century were designed to be fitted with optional lamps so that they could be used as newel-post lights. In this manner, it was not difficult at all for the man of average means to afford the drama of a light standard in his hallway. And if you have the newel post, even today you can illuminate it with a fixture such as this one from **Victorian Light-crafters.** Model N100 is 16″ wide and 28″ high. The shades illustrated are etched glass with amber rims; many other styles are available, as well.

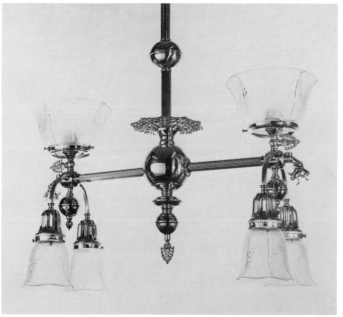

1, 2, 3. Victorian Lightcrafters makes all of its solid-brass reproductions to order, enabling the customer to specify length. At top left is its model C625, 26″ wide and from 26″ to 50″ long. Available with either two or four arms, it is fitted with clear pressed-glass shades, though a variety of styles is available to suit individual taste. Model C311, at top right, comes with either four or six arms. Opalescent swirl shades with ruffled edges complement the ornate detailing of the brasswork. Clear etched-glass shades with amber rims adorn this four- or six-arm model (bottom, left). Length ranges from 24″ to 44″; width is 29″. Specify number C751.

4. The thought of cleaning the intricate brasswork on this lavishly embellished combination chandelier might be daunting, were it not for the fact that model GES 2-4, like all of **Roy Electric**'s fixtures, is lacquered. All you'll need is a damp cloth to keep it sparkling. With that in mind, the only really difficult task you'll have is deciding how many arms you'd like it to have, and what length is appropriate for its use.

5

6

8

7

9

The handsome brass combination wall fixtures pictured here are far removed in both concept and execution from the primitive, though no less attractive, candle sconces which were their ancestors. Each has its place in a period home, though the Victorian fixture will be more costly to install if you're not already blessed with a junction box in just the right place. Since these sconces are all totally wired for electricity, at least you won't have to worry about installing gas lines as well. **5. M-H Lamp & Fan Company**'s model 8303 is fitted with a satin-etched electric shade and a pressed-glass gas shade. Such eclecticism, one of the hallmarks of Victorian design, makes the piece even more authentic. **6. M-H Lamp**'s style 8324 is shown here with floral, feminine-looking shades. The handsome rope tubing would complement any number of shade styles, however, and a different choice would give the fixture a very different look. **7.** Two simple sconces from **Victorian Reproductions** are virtually unadorned. As such, either would complement a more opulent existing chandelier, or would be an interesting counterpoint to the exuberant patterns and colors so typical of Victorian papers and paints. **8, 9.** While these two combination sconces from **Victorian Lightcrafters** are identical in basic construction, each having twin electric lights and a single, larger gas light, they are quite different in appearance. Model W290 (left) has more elaborate brasswork, while model W265 (right) is less dramatic in its use of ornament. (Note, however, that the holders for the shades are common to both sconces.)

Early Electric Fixtures

In 1879, after months of fruitless experiments, Thomas Alva Edison succeeded in making an incandescent lamp in which a loop of carbonized cotton thread glowed in a vacuum for over forty hours. Thus began a lighting revolution that led eventually to the wiring of the world. The benefits of electric light were immediately recognized—illumination at the turn of a knob, with no fuel fonts to fill, no wicks to clean, no smoke to soil draperies and walls. But one initially startling innovation of Edison's invention is almost lost on us today. For the first time in history, the source of light could be directed downward as well as up. As a result, many early electric fixtures, taking full advantage of this dramatic novelty, looked like nothing that had come before them. Only recently reviled as hopelessly old-fashioned, early electric fixtures are now reproduced in abundance for residents of period houses and apartments.

1, 2. The craftsmen at **Victorian Reproductions** spent a decade repairing and maintaining original Victorian fixtures before turning their talents to the creation of expert reproductions such as the two chandeliers shown here. The first, a twin-armed early electric fixture, is noteworthy for the elaborate scrollwork which flanks its central pendant. The detailing in the brasswork of the single-light fixture is echoed by the ruffled edges and decorative etching of its pretty glass shade. **3. Crawford's Old House Store** is a one-stop shopping center for both reproduction lighting fixtures and accessories and for period hardware, decorative items, and plumbing fixtures as well. Each item in its catalogue is covered by a money-back guarantee, making

1

2

3

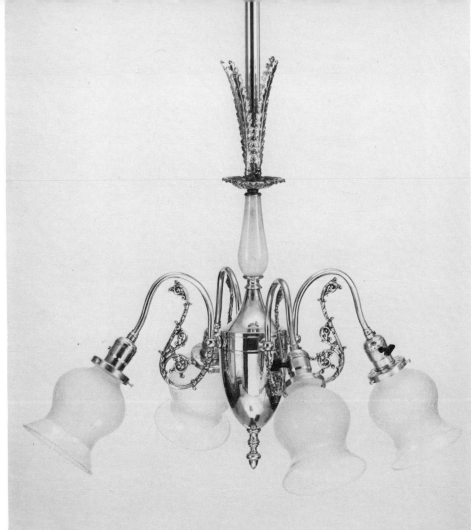

4

selection a much more reassuring
task. This single-light ceiling fixture
is crafted of solid brass and finished with a cut-glass shade in a
ruby tint. **4.** An elaborate, four-
armed electric chandelier from **Victorian Reproductions** would be
equally effective hung over a dining
table or in an entrance hall. **5.** Were
for the elaborate scrollwork which
is one of the hallmarks of Victorian
design, one might almost take this
billiard or conference table
chandelier for a modern fixture.
Crawford's Old House Store includes green cased-glass shades with
this ceiling fixture, which measures
48″ wide and 34″ high.

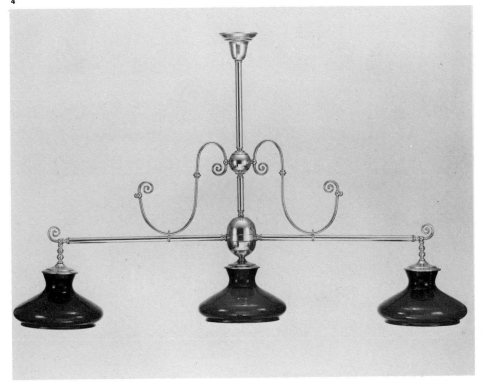

5

84

1

2

3

1. Liberty, a formal nine-light chandelier from **Illuminating Experiences,** features ornate detailing and polished gold finish. **2.** Cased glass cones are shown on **Classic Illumination**'s model 1904-4, but a wide variety of additional shades are available. **3, 4. Brasslight**'s Turnhouse and Europa are illustrative of the wide variety of styles made possible by the use of electricity. Turnhouse features five delicate hand-blown glass shades; Europa, available in two- or three-arm models, is fitted with small cased-glass cones. **5. Nowell**'s Old Waldorf is an elegant five-light parlor fixture. Choose polished or antique brass finish and a length of from 15″ to 39″ overall. **6. Victorian Lightcrafters** will make its model C975 with from two to six arms. Total length can be varied from 19″ to 49″. **7.** Bully Boy would be a good choice over a billiard table. **Brasslight** offers the model with large cased-glass cones; dimensions are 29″ by 35″. **8.** This custom design by Richard P. Donohoe for **Washington Copper Works** is an adaptation of the Arts and Crafts style popular in the early 20th century. **9.** The lovely scrollwork on **Victorian Lightcrafters'** model C-201 is a nice counterpoint to its scalloped-edged shades. As are so many of the firm's designs, it is available with from two to six arms. **10. Roy Electric** is noted for its flexibility in chandelier manufacture; the company will produce any of its stock models in a size to suit the customer. Number EC 3-8, shown here, can be ordered with rope, reeded, or plain brass tubing, as can the firm's other designs. **11, 12, 13. Victorian Lightcrafters** produces some of its brass chandeliers using casts from antique fixtures. Most are offered in two- to six-arm models, with a choice of shades and of tubing styles (either rope, reeded, or plain). Shown in illustrations 11, 12, and 13 are model numbers C-420, C-920, and C-880, respectively.

4

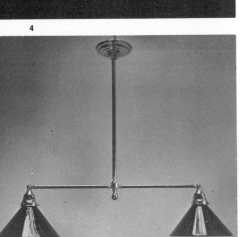

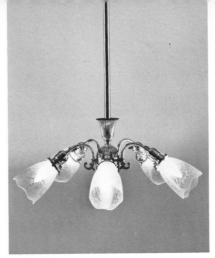

5

8

11

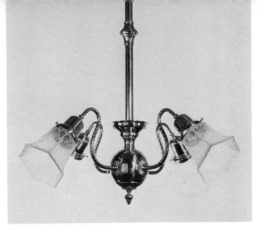

6

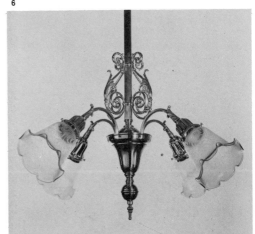

9

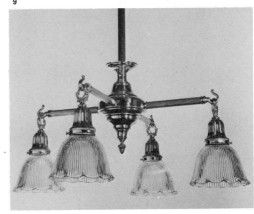

12

13

1

2

3

Many of the early electric wall sconces shown here are styled to match chandeliers illustrated on the previous four pages. But any of them would look equally well used alone. **1, 2, 3. Victorian Light-crafters** will supply any of its solid-brass sconces in either polished and lacquered finish, antiqued and lacquered finish, or natural polished brass which attains a lovely patina as it ages. All accommodate standard 60-watt bulbs; choose rope, reeded, or plain tubing. Shown here are the firm's models W975-3, W420, and W975. **4. M-H Lamp & Fan Company**'s model 8306 is an unadorned style that would suit any number of decorating schemes. It extends just 8″ from the wall. **5.** Model SED 3-3 from **Roy Electric** is a triple-armed sconce with a graceful oval wall plate. **6. Brasslight**'s Cedar Hill sconce is shown here with a delicately ruffled shade. The design is also offered in a two- or three-arm chandelier. **7.** Model 8331S from **M-H Lamp & Fan** would be a good choice in a narrow hallway; it extends only 6″ from the wall. The fixture takes a standard 60-watt bulb and is available with your choice of shade. **8.** The roped tubing used for the gracefully arched twin arms of **Roy Electric** model SED 2-2 is echoed in the ornamentation of the oval wall plate. The fixture is shown with pressed-glass shades. **9. Brasslight**'s Turnhouse sconce features a serpentine arm and a ribbed pressed-glass shade. A matching chandelier is also offered. **10.** Although **Roy Electric** is best known for its reproduction Victorian chandeliers, the company's expertise is evident in simpler wall sconces as well. Model SED 1-2 is a twin-armed fixture with a simple, oval wall plate.

4

5

6

8

7

9

10

Early electric hanging fixtures such as the ones shown on this page are less elaborate than the first electrified chandeliers, and thus better suited to informal surroundings. **1.** Model C-125 from **Victorian Lightcrafters** is 16″ wide and from 11″ to 30″ long. Its three lights are fitted with ribbed pressed-glass shades. **2.** Grape Trellis is one of **Progress Lighting**'s Tiffany-style fixtures. Hundreds of pieces of hand-foiled glass are assembled to make the 21″-diameter shade. **3. Crawford's Old House Store** fits this chain-hung lamp with a white satin glass shade (ask for model 8815-1). **4. Classic Illuminations'** stock number 1920-1 is a reproduction of an electrolier made around 1920. Three brass rods support the handsome etched-glass dish shade. **5.** A graceful ribbed-glass shade is all the adornment needed on **Roy Electric**'s model P1E1. Adaptable to any standard ceiling height, it can be ordered in lengths ranging from 12″ to 42″. **6.** One of the Liberty series from **Illuminating Experiences**, this ceiling fixture is embellished by richly detailed cast antique brasswork and by its satin-etched shade which features a butterfly motif. **7, 8.** The juxtaposition of these two table lamps with the early electric ceiling fixtures which precede them may seem strange until you realize that both are careful reproductions of contemporaneous designs by the prescient Frank Lloyd Wright. The two-pedestal art glass lamp was especially created for Wright's famous Robie House (Chicago, 1909). Wright's Prairie Lamp looks deceptively simple; there are, however, 64 separate pieces involved in its manufacture. Both of these handsome designs have been painstakingly reproduced by **Heinz & Company**.

1

2

3

5

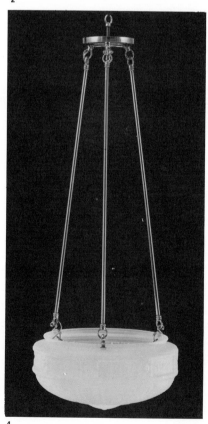

4

6

7

8

1

No black-and-white illustration, no matter its clarity, can do justice to the superb table lamps shown here, for their luminous colors are a large part of their appeal. **1.** These three extraordinary lamps are modern interpretations of the work of Émile Gallé, a leading exponent of the Art Nouveau style in the late 19th century. Designed and handcrafted by de Vianne for **Sierra Trading Company,** each is composed of multiple layers of colored glass, surface-etched to create a three-dimensional quality. **2. Calger Lighting**'s model A1-2093 features a matching hand-blown Venetian glass shade and column. Fittings are solid brass, and the total height is 22″. The glowing colors are primarily shades of orange and yellow. **3, 4, 5. Lyn Hovey** is that rarest of combinations—both artist and craftsman. His skills with stained glass are such that he and his associates have been called upon to handle delicate

2

restoration work, not only on windows by most of America's famous studios (including Tiffany and LaFarge) but on early European panels as well. Admirers of Tiffany's wonderful lampshades need not pine over the scarcity of his work today; they can contact Hovey for one of his own (signed) original designs, any one of which even Tiffany might envy. The table lamps and hanging fixtures shown here range in size from 10½″ to 18″ in diameter. Patterns illustrated are the Feather, Diamond, Etched Rose, Iris, Day Lily, and Peacock. This last is a particular favorite of the artist's, and rightly so, for it is composed of nearly 500 pieces of glass, and the colors are iridescent, with blues and greens predominating.

3

4

5

1. The **Sierra Trading Company** desk and piano lamps pictured above are certainly more modest than the elegant glass creations shown on the previous pages. But they are no less useful and no less representative of styles indigenous to the early electric age. At the top are a three-arm rope-brass table lamp with cast-brass base and two-arm piano lamps with cased-glass shades. They range in height from 15″ to 17½″. At center are a single and a double gooseneck, flanking a piano lamp which swivels at both top and bottom. And, finally, three desk lamps, representative of those designed around the turn of the century for use by accountants. Each is 12½″ high; the shades are cased glass in tones of coffee or green. Any would make a good period accent on a desk or side table where space is at a premium.

Kerosene Lamps

When petroleum, from which kerosene is derived, was discovered in Pennsylvania in 1859, it not only created a new wave of American millionaires, but it also provided an endless source of oil for the nation's lamps. Kerosene burns brightly, is relatively clean, and, because of its abundance, is unusually cheap. As a continuous stream of improvements perfected the efficiency of kerosene burners, kerosene lamps became the primary mode of lighting in North America during the second half of the 19th century. No matter the other means of lighting used in the Victorian home, kerosene lamps were always present. Hanging kerosene lamps developed as fashionable imitations of the centrally-fixed gasolier. Once gas chandeliers became popular, hanging kerosene lamps became the vogue where gas was inaccessible or unaffordable. Today electrified adaptations of hanging kerosene lamps are made by a number of suppliers, while portable kerosene lamps in clear glass, made from original molds, are readily available in country hardware stores.

3

4

2. **Victorian Reproductions** makes this electrified kerosene lamp reproduction in its own shop, as it does all of its fixtures. 3. **Progress Lighting**'s chain-hung lamp would be a perfect choice for a "country-look" dining room. It takes a three-way bulb, is fitted with a hobnail glass shade, and has an antique brass finish. 4. Fratino, designed by Sciolari of Rome for **Illuminating Experiences,** is gleaming solid brass with an opal glass shade.

Decorated Glass Shades

What makes a Victorian or Edwardian lighting fixture pleasing to the eye is not merely the outline of its shape or the materials from which it is made, but the play of light against the surface of its decorated shades. Victorian glassmakers were masters of the art of designing and decorating chimneys, globes, and shades as fixtures of every lighting mode were introduced and improved upon. By the 1880s, when high-style décor reached the apex of ornateness, shades, and even the lamp chimneys within, sported etched or painted designs and crimped and tinted edges. Today's reproduction experts, heirs of yesterday's glassmakers, offer as wide a variety as was manufactured in the past, their wares often made from original molds.

Roy Electric's specialty is the creation of elaborate brass chandeliers in sizes to suit the customer's specifications, no matter how unusual they may be. The company has many Victorian and early 20th-century styles that it offers as stock items, or will recreate a client's design upon request. There are times, however, when your needs may be simpler. Even if all you need is a gas or electric shade to replace a broken one on a treasured antique, Roy Electric can probably supply it. Pictured here are just a few of the glass shades in stock.
1. These six shades are meant for early electric fixtures. On the top row, from left to right, are three

1

2

3

4

acid-etched shades, each with a fitter measuring 2¼". The first, in frosted glass, measures 5" by 5". The second, in frosted or amber glass, is 4½" wide and 5½" high; the last, again in frosted glass, is 5¼" wide by 4¼" high. On the bottom row, from left to right, are an amber or frosted acid-etched shade, 5" by 4¼" with a 2¼" fitter; a frosted acid-etched shade, 5" by 8" with a 3¼" fitter; and a blue swirl shade of the same dimensions. **2.** The four shades illustrated here are intended for gas fixtures. On the top row are a lovely globe of acid-etched frosted glass, 9" by 8½" with a 4" fitter and a gracefully scalloped etched-glass shade available with an amber rim, cranberry rim, or frosted. It measures 5½" by 5" and has a 4" fitter. Below, left, are a pressed-glass shade in clear or amber, measuring 7½" by 4", and an acid-etched frosted shade, 7¼" by 4½". Each has a 4" fitter. **3.** Another quartet of gas shades all have 4" fitters and measure roughly 7¼" by 4". At top left is an acid-etched shade with amber rim; on the right, a frosted glass shade, also acid etched. The scalloped shade on the bottom row combines both frosted and clear pressed glass; the last is available in either amber or acid-etched frosted glass. **4.** All of the electric shades pictured here have 2¼" fitters; none is wider than 5", making them ideal for smaller fixtures. Of the six, five are made of acid-etched glass, the exception being the shade at the upper right, which is pressed-glass available in a frosted/clear combination or in an amber tint.

The renewed interest in Victoriana has brought about a minor business boom in the lighting hardware industry. Glass shades, many made from original molds, are now available in a profusion of designs that rival the contents of 19th-century lighting catalogues. Shown here are further examples of glass shades made today. Still, they represent only a few of the hundreds of reproduction shades on the current market. **1, 2. Victorian Lightcrafters** not only restores and sells antique lighting fixtures, but also has its own line of quality reproductions in solid brass. In addition, the company stocks a number of etched and pressed-glass shades in various sizes and colors to fit gas, electric, or combination gas and electric fixtures. The three pressed-glass shades shown in the top row have 2¼″ fitters and range in width from 4½″ to 6″ and in height from 4″ to 4½″. The second row shows a trio of 4″ fitters. At the left is a simple pressed-glass model; in the center and at right, two gracefully etched designs. The heights range from 4″ to 5½″, the width from 7″ to 8½″. **3, 4. M-H Lamp & Fan Company**'s major business is the manufacture of solid-brass lighting reproductions from the Victorian and Edwardian periods. The firm also offers a complete restoration service for antique ceiling fans and lighting fixtures, and stocks a number of lead crystal glass shades for early fixtures. Shown here are just a few of the models available, in fitter sizes ranging from 2¼″ to 4″. **5, 6, 7.** No matter whether you require a single simply cut shade for a small wall sconce or a dozen ornate fitters for an elaborate gas and

1

2

3

4

5

6

7

electric chandelier, chances are that **Victorian Reproductions** will have just what you are looking for. Shown here are just a few styles from the company's catalogue. Many of the shades are available in more than one size, and they range in design from an unadorned clear glass globe to an elaborately scalloped, cut-glass piece. Making the right selection won't be easy, but it should be a lot of fun.

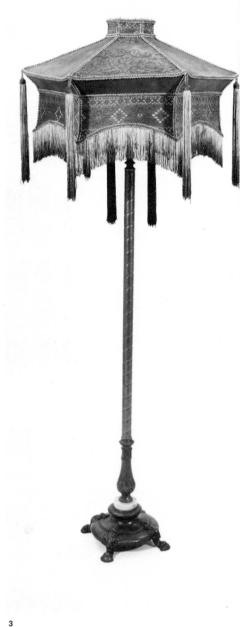

1

2

3

If you are among the many devotees of the lush, opulent Victorian style, you'll probably have discovered that it's difficult to find certain items that are true both to the letter and spirit of that extravagant age in interior decoration. Lampshades such as these fringed beauties, for instance, are not readily available at your local department store or lighting retailer.

Thank goodness for the entrepreneurs who recognized the need for these fantastic decorative touches of the late 19th and early 20th centuries and who are able to reproduce them so expertly! **1, 2, 3.** Esther Rister creates her own designs for **Yestershades**, using silks, satins, georgettes, velvets, and antique laces. Since each shade is made entirely by hand and the

fabrics are often dyed to suit customer specifications, no two are ever exactly alike. Three of Rister's Victorian fantasies are pictured here; many others are available as well, and custom work is welcomed. **4.** Gail Teller's designs for **The Shade Tree** are certainly very different from the beaded, fringed fabric shades pictured elsewhere on these two pages, but they are no

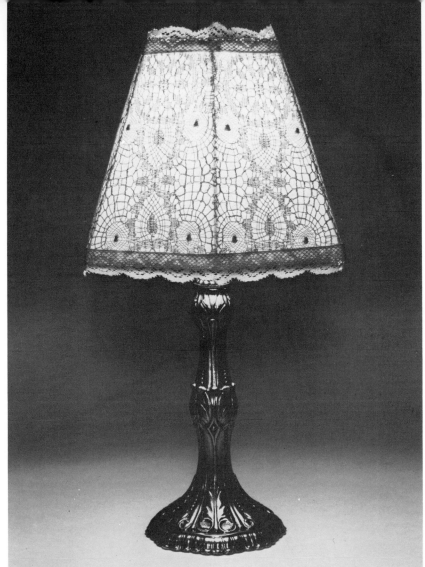

5

6

7

less original in either concept or in execution. Teller hand crafts cut and pierced shades such as this one on parchment paper; each is fully lined to protect the cuts and diffuse the light evenly. **5. The Elegant Cat** is appropriately housed in a century-old Victorian inn, proper inspiration for its elegant period shades. Empress, shown here, is 14½″ in diameter and 19″ high, including its lavishly applied fringe of glass beads. (A fabric fringe can be substituted if desired). Suitable for either a floor or table lamp, this particular design is primarily red in color. Custom colors are available for all of the company's designs. **6.** This lovely scalloped shade is the work of **The Shade Tree.** Gail Teller offers a variety of patterns to suit every taste, from birds, wild flowers, vines, and grasses to geometric figures, boats, and buildings. She will hand-cut, stencil, or paint the designs you choose on a lampshade the proper style and size for your fixture. **7.** Tracy Holcomb of **Shades of the Past** works with silk to create original, hand-sewn designs such as this one. Lotus, 15″ in diameter and 14″ tall, is available in a variety of colors, with fringe and trim dyed to match and contrasting tassels. Custom work is welcomed.

Art Deco Lighting

Dismissed, even in the 1920s and '30s, as trash or kitsch by people of conservative taste, Art Deco has achieved an almost fanatic popularity in our time that was virtually undreamed of in its own. Art Deco was a style that consciously strove for modernity and an artistic expression to complement the machine age. Essentially a style of decoration, it favored low-relief geometrical designs, often in the form of parallel straight lines, zigzags, chevrons, and stylized floral motifs. In lighting fixtures, as in furnishings, the style displayed a dramatic bias for the horizontal; the natural verticality of a hanging fixture, for example, would almost always be offset by strong horizontal elements. With Art Deco lighting almost *de rigueur* in today's postmodern settings, period fixtures are beginning to crowd the catalogues of contemporary lighting manufacturers.

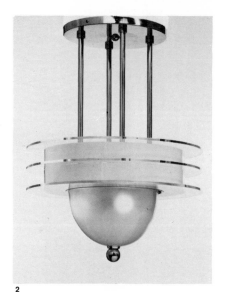

2

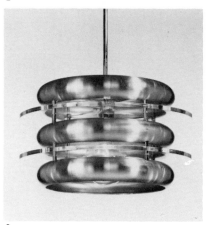

3

1

1. This streamlined **Paul Hanson** chandelier is composed of white satin glass shades fitted into polished brass arms; the central column is finished in black lacquer, or you may opt for Milan red lacquer or all-brass finish. **2.** A stylish ceiling fixture from **Metropolitan Lighting** features a rotund glass diffuser whose lines are echoed by three Plexiglas rings above it. Total height, including the brass columns and circular ceiling plate, is 25″. **3.** Brushed aluminum circlets are interspersed with clear Plexiglas discs and accented with polished chrome in this **Metropolitan Lighting** offering. 21″ in diameter, it takes one 150-watt bulb. **4.** A potpourri of Art Deco styles is avail-

able from **Paul Hanson.** To the left are two polished brass torchieres, the tallest 70″ high. In the center is a Milan red and polished brass table lamp with matching red shade; on the right, two polished brass and lacquer (ivory or black) floor lamps, both 70″ tall. **5.** Capiz shell from the Philippines forms the diffuser of this striking wall sconce from **Illuminating Experiences. 6.** Polished chrome, unadorned save for a ribbed pattern at its center, is depended from clear glass rods in a striking ceiling fixture from **Metropolitan Lighting. 7.** Any of these sleek sconces would add just the right Art Deco touch to a wall, whether used singly or in groups. **Metropolitan Lighting** uses a variety of materials—polished brass, polished chrome, white Lucite, and satin aluminum—for these designs, which range in height from about 6″ to nearly 24″.

4

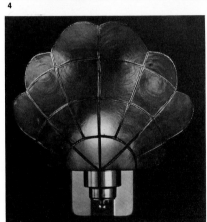

5

6

7

Traditional Lighting

When anyone active in the world of home furnishings speaks of traditional styling, he has in mind a mode of design that is neither antique nor modern, a style that is "safe" and "neutral" because it lacks both the curatorial correctness of the antique and the ostentatious drama of the modern. Traditional lighting fixtures, like traditional furniture, are decorative hybrids, the issue of a marriage between the old and the new. Old shapes, already classics in the distant past, are modeled from long-established materials to create a decidedly *new* object—different from anything that could have existed in the past and different from the shapes adopted by the avant-garde and called modern. Thus, the turned-brass candlestick of the 18th century is adapted by the traditional designer, its proportions subtly altered, its base replaced by a jade plinth, its candle socket made to accommodate a three-way bulb, the length of its candle dictating the height of a harp, and the whole crowned by a hand-shirred muslin shade. Or the brass English chandelier of the same historic period is translated into delft, with each arm capped by a handsomely proportioned parchment shade that would have been unthinkable in an age of candlelight but is eminently suitable for an incandescent bulb.

Like marriage in general, design compatability can yield wonderful results. But the union of unlike entities can be doomed to failure. How else can one explain the large numbers of deformed monsters, born of commerce and cheap materials, that are palmed off on us as "traditional"—bulbous shapes, hideous colors, malformed shades—eyesores that are found in many living rooms across the continent?

The traditional lighting fixtures that follow are largely uncommon. You will not ordinarily find them in your local lighting showroom or in the average department store, even though their materials, while fine, are entirely familiar: cut crystal, hand-blown glass, hand-painted porcelain, and solid brass. The table lamps in particular are magnificently proportioned, with shades of chintz, muslin, parchment, and shantung that complement the bases with pleasing shapes and colors. As you will discover, the traditional need not be conventional.

Opposite page: A sophisticated brass-trimmed glass column is topped with a gray-toned mushroom-pleated shade in this sleek traditional design from Beth Weissman Company.

Traditional Table Lamps

Traditional table lamps can be purchased almost anywhere.
And that's the problem with them. Most look as if they *were*
bought anywhere. The same basic forms—ginger jar, brass
candlestick, crystal vase—are seemingly the law of the land, as
if by statutory decree all department stores were obliged to sell
the same five lamps with the same ribbed paper shades to an
unenlightened public. Let the table lamps that follow—all
handsomely proportioned and with a variety of shades—break
a merchandising conspiracy that has gone unquestioned far
too long.

The 61-year-old firm of **Beth
Weissman** has an international
reputation for traditional lamps and
chandeliers of high quality. The
designs of the company's table
lamps originate in France, Italy,
and Germany; many of them are
embellished by the Weissman staff
and made in the company's own
factory. Weissman lamps are true
lifetime investments and superb ad-
ditions to a carefully planned
design scheme. Among the company's many fine table lamps
represented in this book are the five
shown on these two pages.

1

1. Smooth lines and simple shapes compose this exceptional design. A black parchment shade tops a satin-glass pyramid body connected by circles of brass to a base of shining chrome. The overall height is 29″; the shade measures 10″ square at the base, 5½″ square at the top, and 15½″ tall. **2.** Hand-blown glass illustrating the fine art of decoupage features silvery Art-Nouveau nudes on a black satin surface. Mounted on a solid-brass base, it is crowned by a variegated pleated shade in ascot gray and soars to a height of 27½″. **3.** Lustrous hand-cut Italian lead crystal with a traditional bird and wheat motif is mounted on an oval brass plate over an octagonal brass base. The off-white shade is made of shirred shantung. This elegant design is 24½″ tall. **4.** A bell-shaped hurricane lamp imported from France features a striking Art Nouveau design on frosted glass. Beautifully mounted on a double base of solid brass, the fixture is 16″ tall. **5.** Exquisite symmetry and detailing are evident in this French hand-painted ceramic vase supported by a three-pronged solid-brass base. The champagne-toned mushroom-pleated shade is trimmed to match the principal color of the vase, a rich oxblood which recalls the more earthy and primitive terra cotta of ancient times. The overall effect of this 25½″-tall fixture, however, is anything but primitive.

2

3

4

5

1

Founded in 1920, the **Paul Hanson Company** enjoys a deserved reputation as a leading importer and manufacturer of lamps, chandeliers, and desk accessories. The firm's designers work closely with artisans around the world who interpret their ideas in porcelain, ceramic, crystal, and glass. Hanson's own foundry produces brass mountings and accessories; it also operates its own woodworking facility. Each lamp is crafted by hand and assembled from start to finish by one person to assure continuity.

2

3

1. A traditional ginger jar lamp is interpreted in soft green ceramic porcelain with a brass finial and a solid-brass base resting on four scrolled feet. The shade is linen. **2.** A handsome two-candle desk lamp features a glossy deep green shade trimmed with accents which match its solid-brass base. **3.** The passion for the Art Nouveau and Art Deco styles of the early 20th century is enjoying a deserved revival; this lamp is obviously part of the trend. Ribs of black porcelain on gray are complemented by a pale gray butcher linen shade, the whole 26″ high. **4.** A delicate floral motif features soft green, violet, and earth-toned accents on off white. The vase is trimmed in brass and rests on a solid-brass base; a shantung shade completes the look of elegance.

4

A dozen more of **Beth Weissman**'s beautifully crafted interpretations of the traditional table lamp are shown on these two pages. The variety of materials and styles is self-evident; the quality is unsurpassed. **1.** No doubt inspired by the classic brass candlestick, this well-tailored, handsome desk lamp features a black parchment shade which mirrors the lines of its octagonal base. The overall height is 24½″. **2.** One look at this unusual lamp will remind you of New York City's architectural masterpiece of the Art Deco period, the Chrysler Building. And the resemblance is carried further by its ceramic finish of fired gold and antique silver. The lamp rests on a brass plate and a foundation of black wood, balanced by a black parchment shade, the whole 24″ high. **3.** Fine Limoges porcelain composes this handsome black fluted vase. The trimming is hand-applied 18-karat gold and sienna; the shade, hand-sewn of ivory shantung. **4.** Brilliantly polished brass accents the classic lines of this formal lamp. Smoothly fluted corners soften its rectangular lines; a legged octagonal base is offset by an unusual corner-pleated shade of champagne-colored shantung. **5.** A hand-cut tapered lead crystal column imported from Germany is imprinted with a thumbprint design. The 30½″-tall lamp is complemented by a shade of pleated pearl gray muslin. **6.** Rattan lacquered in a deep tobacco hue is paired with solid-brass accents. The stem rests on a brass square mounted on a wood base and is topped by a mushroom-colored

1

2

3

4

5

6

7

8

pleated shade. **7.** The classic vase is interpreted here in hand-blown ribbed glass imported from Italy. Known as case glass, it is actually two types of glass, soft pastel opal glass bonded to satin glass for an interesting effect. Placed on a brass base, the lamp is 17″ tall. **8.** A putty-colored pleated shade in an unusual rectangular shape tops two four-sided, gracefully tapered brass columns. Mounted on a handsome base of black lacquered wood and brass, the fixture is 20″ in overall height. **9.** The ordinary desk lamp becomes extraordinary when interpreted in clear lucite and brass. The crowning touch is an apricot satin glass shade. **10.** This uncommon lamp is both a useful lighting device and a beautiful piece of abstract sculpture. The sinuous brass form is mounted on a black and clear lucite base and has a linen-textured knife-pleated shade. It is 29″ tall. **11.** The finest Wedgwood forms this handsome black jasperware vase. It is finished with an alternate-pleated shantung shade. **12.** A fluted pedestal brass base supports an elegant egg shape hand-decorated in earth tones. The shade is putty-colored butcher linen, pleated in a variegated style.

9

10

11

12

1

2

3

4

5

1. There are numerous settings in which these handmade stoneware lamps would look just right. Designed by George Scatchard for **George Kovacs**, they are available in white, sand, or charcoal. Each takes a three-way bulb with a maximum power of 250 watts. Fitted with teak necks and shirred natural muslin shades, they are 16″ and 20″ tall. **2.** Ranging in height from 16½″ to 29″, these Scatchard stoneware fixtures offered by **George Kovacs** come in a wide range of colors certain to complement almost any décor: matte white, gloss black, blue, or green, iron red, earth tone, sand, and charcoal. Each takes a three-way bulb (maximum 250 watts). The shade is pleated oyster linen. **3. Baldwin Hardware** has 35 years' experience in creating beautiful brass accessories for the home. These lamps are adaptations of colonial fixtures found in some of America's finest historical museums and are fitted with black parchment shades with hand-rolled edges or white pleated muslin shades. **4. Koch & Lowy**'s well-named Acropolis features three sleek columns of polished brass or chrome topped by a beige or white linen shade. The handsome lamp is 30″ tall; it can also be ordered in a floor model and accommodates two 100-watt bulbs. **5.** The mythical griffin is featured in this **Classic Illumination** reproduction of a Victorian library lamp first made around 1875 and now adapted for contemporary homes. Offered in solid brass with lacquer or dark lacquer finish, it is fitted with two 60-watt candelabra-base bulbs. The black shade has a white interior and a rolled gold edge; the lamp is 24″ tall.

1

Traditional Floor Lamps

For too long the torchiere or decorative floor lamp was relegated to the attic, a legacy of the Depression when, like the *Normandie*, it added a touch of luxury to dark times or as a holdback from the '40s when it came in wooden models with parchment shades and stood awkwardly in maple or blonde-wood bedroom suites. With the revival of interest in Art Deco, and especially with the trendy onset of eclectic postmodernism, the torchiere has returned to popularity with a vengeance. Here are some of the best models available today, all designed for the traditional interior.

Classic, beautifully proportioned floor lamps are a **Beth Weissman** hallmark, as these four examples indicate. **1.** A brushed steel column bisected by its own glass table is fitted to a polished brass base. The 56″ fixture has a black parchment shade. **2.** Rattan on a hexagonal brass base is topped by a hand-sewn, mushroom-pleated butcher linen shade. **3, 4.** Both of these solid-brass lamps are fitted with glass shades and touch-light control. The fluted shade is cased glass in gray and mauve; the other, hand-blown cut crystal and satin glass.

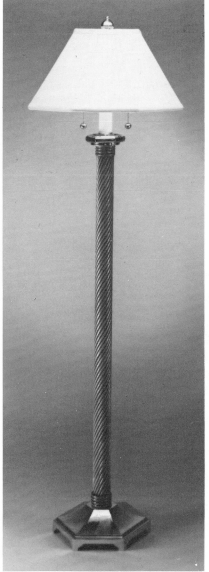

2

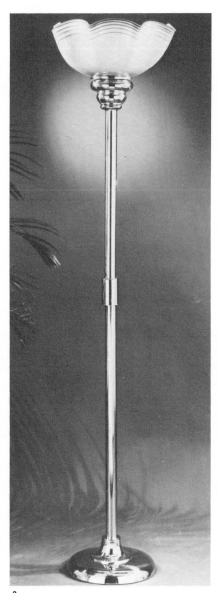

3

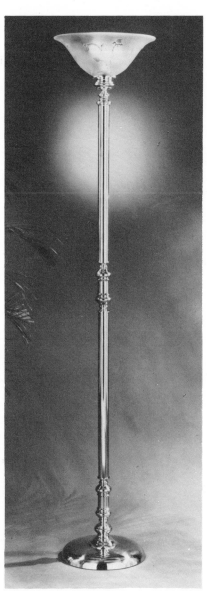

4

Traditional Hanging and Ceiling Lamps

Some people think that the word *traditional* is synonymous with *commonplace* or even *boring*. True, traditional decor is too much with us—in tony advertisements, in the model rooms of department stores, in the living rooms of our maiden aunts, in the showrooms of most home furnishing stores. Still, because it is ubiquitous, the look of traditional comfort and grace so prized by most of us is singularly difficult to achieve successfully, particularly in lighting fixtures that depend from or affix to the ceiling. The fixtures sold at roadside lighting centers are all too predictable: swag lamps guaranteed to exude the ambience of motel rooms and amber chandeliers suggesting diners pretending to be restaurants. Let the pages that follow prove the refreshingly varied array of traditional styles available to the demanding consumer.

1

1. Metropolitan Lighting offers this ornate, formal chandelier, two tiers of gold-plated cast bronze and Bohemian crystal to illuminate an elegant entrance hall or dining room. **2. Illuminating Experiences'** graceful chandelier is composed of gold-plated cast brass and satin-etched hand-blown glass. **3.** A gleaming solid-brass chandelier from **Beth Weissman** is 34″ in diameter. Black parchment shades are lined with gold foil. **4.** The arms of this solid-brass chandelier from **Paul Hanson** are shaped to resemble French horns. The hanging tassels are an added touch. **5.** Peter Hamburger designed this acrylic and polished-brass hanging lamp for **George Kovacs**. The shades are stretched natural muslin. **6.** Model P5032 from **Progress Lighting** has a beveled glass shade protecting a glass globe. The accents are brass. **7.** Simulated wicker with antique brass-finish trim is offered by **Progress Lighting** in several styles. **8.** The classic style of this 12-arm chandelier from **Paul Hanson** would complement a variety of traditional interiors. **9.** A gleaming brass column supports five gold-banded opal glass shades in this simply styled fixture from **Progress Lighting**. **10.** The largest of a number of similarly designed fixtures offered by **Illuminating Experiences** can be ordered in amber or clear hand-blown glass. It is 16″ in diameter. **11.** Champagne-colored hand-blown glass is fashioned into graceful wild flowers in this fanciful design from **Illuminating Experiences**. It takes five frosted candelabra-base bulbs.

2

3

4

5

6

7

8

9

10 ◄

11 ►

1

2

3

4

5

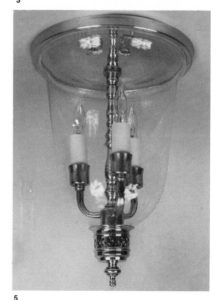

Flush-mounted ceiling fixtures are sometimes the only solution for small spaces; it doesn't mean, however, that such a solution has to involve the ordinary inverted glass "plates" so commonly installed in the traditional home today. **1. Illuminating Experiences** offers several circular fixtures which feature detailed cast-brass mountings and either clear pressed diamond glass or satin-etched and clear glass diffusers. **2.** Polished brass with glass or cut crystal globes come in sizes from 8″ to 16″ in diameter; from **Metropolitan Lighting. 3.** The Pub Light from **Washington Copper Works** is 12½″ wide by 6½″ high. Available in untreated or stained copper, it takes three round bulbs in its candelabra sockets. **4. Progress Lighting**'s hexagonal ceiling light comes in polished or antique brass with beveled clear glass panels. Its dimensions are 13″ by 6¼″. **5, 6. William Spencer** carries several handsome ceiling fixtures. The two shown here, Houghton (*opposite page*) and Vincentown, are both offered in polished or antique brass or pewter finish with hand-blown glass globes. Each takes three candelabra-base bulbs. **7. Newstamp Lighting**'s hexagonal ceiling light is fashioned of solid brass (in polished or antique brass finish), fitted with clear beveled glass. A smoky tint eliminates glare from its three bulbs. **8. Progress Lighting**'s triple-globe fixture is offered in antique or polished brass, oak with brass, or almond finish. Three 60-watt bulbs are needed; the fixture overall is 15″ in diameter and 7¾″ high.

6

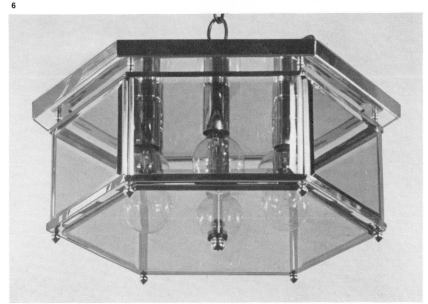

7

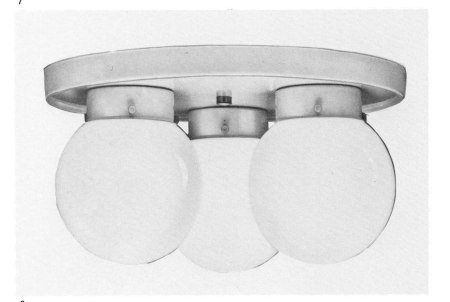

8

117

3.

Modern Lighting

Lighting is more than a convenience. A room can be shaped by light placement; it will affect the room's colors, dimension, and comfort. Poor lighting can make a beautifully outfitted room gloomy and unwelcoming. Clever lighting, on the other hand, will hide a room's defects and awkward elements and create an inviting space.

Modern lighting fixtures go one step further: they are often decorative elements in themselves. Some of today's lighting designs, notably those from Italian studios, are virtually sculptures that also happen to provide illumination. Modern designers tend to make use of classic forms fabricated in up-to-date materials—chrome, steel, aluminum, thermoplastics, and rubber—as well as in the more traditional glass, brass, and bronze. The styles range from the whimsicality of glass eggs and light columns to the no-nonsense durability of commercial-style track and recessed ceiling lighting.

One of the more exciting innovations in lighting is the trend away from standard incandescent illumination. Fluorescent lighting has advanced a great deal in recent years and is now available in warm color tones and a variety of shapes. With the cost of electricity on the rise, these energy-efficient fixtures should be welcome in residential design. Similarly, halogen and mercury-vapor lamps are coming into wider home use. In addition, modern fixtures are often highly adaptable; they swivel, adjust to different heights, are equipped with dimmers, and can often be mounted or suspended in a variety of ways. Whether you want lighting to make a design statement or simply to illuminate a dark corner, the products described in this chapter cover a broad spectrum of alternatives for the contemporary home and office.

The majority of fixtures that follow are Italian-designed and -made, testimony to a design revolution that has begun to influence the rest of the sophisticated world. But, lest you think that all Italians live in splendid harmony with these gorgeous fixtures, think again. A visit to the average Italian lighting shop will reveal a chamber of horrors equal to our own lighting emporiums. Make no mistake about it: the Italian lighting devices that follow are for design elitists—those who eschew the ordinary and savor the remarkable.

Opposite page: A group of streamlined modern fixtures from Artemide. Called the Aggregato style, the lamps were designed by Enzo Mari and Giancarlo Fassina.

Modern Floor Lamps

The traditional floor lamp, with its metal stanchion and linen or paper shade, was most often placed next to a comfortable, overstuffed armchair in a quiet corner of the living room or den. The combination offered an inviting spot for reading the evening paper or dipping into a good book. Today's sleek designs, though equally suitable for that same purpose, can also be placed more dramatically—in an entrance hall, perhaps, or near a favorite painting or piece of furniture. Contemporary floor lamps are often in themselves as much modern sculpture as they are utilitarian lighting fixtures. In this postmodern era floor lamps are becoming more and more tall and slender. While generally supplying excellent light with halogen bulbs, they are very much artistic experiments in elongated lines. The shades on some models have even been shrinking in order to emphasize the long tubing. A generation addicted to jogging suits and low-caloric meals seems to like its lighting fixtures slender, too.

Interest in contemporary Italian design has never been stronger. Magazines devoted to interior decoration feature the work of Italian artisans on a regular basis and the best that they have to offer is often included in the collection of major museums. The lighting designers at **Artemide** are usually represented in the better collections, as the superbly styled floor lamps by this internationally famous firm and shown on these pages will attest. **1.** Designed by Ernesto Gismondi, the 75″-high Aton is available in white, black, or China red. Equipped with a dimmer switch, it accommodates a 500-watt halogen bulb. **2.** The Callimaco, a creation of Ettore Sottsass, the famed Memphis Group designer, stands 78″ tall; the multicolored lamp is supplied with a 500-watt halogen bulb and dimmer switch. **3.** Gianfranco Frattini's Megaron can be ordered in white, English green, black, or China red. Nearly 72″ tall, the floor model is complemented by an identically styled wall fixture. **4.** Carlo Forcolini's design for the Polifemo incorporates an adjustable circular reflector which not only diffuses the light of the 250-watt halogen bulb downward, but projects interesting patterns on the ceiling as well. This sleek black floor lamp stands nearly 85″ tall. **5.** The Camera 500, another creation of Ernesto Gismondi, is available in both floor and wall models. The floor lamp can be adjusted to heights between 65″ and 76″ and is equipped with a 500-watt halogen bulb and dimmer switch. **6.** Vico Magistretti's Chimera would be a fanciful choice to illuminate even the darkest corner. A mere ⅝″ wide, it is supplied with three 120-watt incandescent tubes along its nearly 72″ length.

1

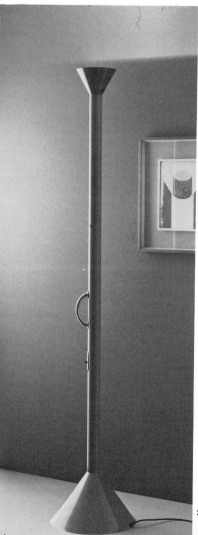

2

3

4

5

6

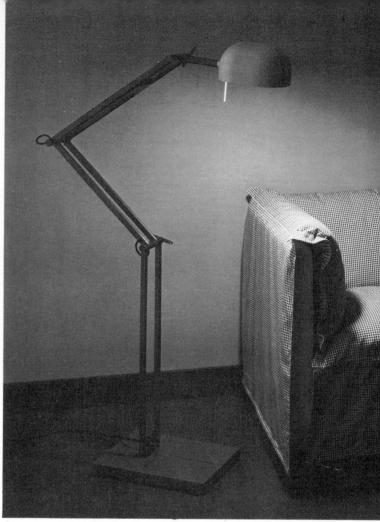

1

2

Avant-garde lighting design is the **Artemide** hallmark, as evidenced by the examples shown on these two pages. Artemide lighting is not for the timid or for those of conservative tastes and would probably look odd in a traditional interior. Any of these floor lamps would be a striking accent in a carefully chosen modern setting, however. Properly placed, each could become the focal point of a room. **1.** Area 50, designed by Mario Bellini, features a variform, adjustable white shade to shield and diffuse the light of a frosted 100-watt bulb. It is available in both 63″ and 82⅝″ heights. **2.** CP & PR Associates created Adone, a fully adjustable gray-painted metal floor lamp with a maximum height of 60⅝″. A 150-watt halogen bulb provides ample light for the most eye-straining of tasks. **3.** The Onfale grouping designed by Luciano Vistosi features hand-blown glass shades. Table models are available in a choice of three sizes—17¼″, 13¼″, and 10¼″; hanging lamps measure 16¾″ and 14″ in diameter. Three 40-watt bulbs illumine the ceiling fixture, while the wall model takes two of the same wattage. The graceful floor lamp extends 71″ in height and is fitted with a 200-watt bulb. **4.** Ernesto Gismondi's Sintesi design can be had in white, black, or red finish and accommodates a 75-watt bulb. It is available in both a fixed model, 57″ tall, and an adjustable one that expands from 57″ to 70″. Sintesi's sleek, minimal styling makes it ideal for rooms where space is at a premium. **5.** Artemide's most successful and recognizable lamp is the Tizio, created in 1971 by Richard Sapper, head designer at IBM. His design has become a modern classic, as witnessed by the fact that it was chosen for the permanent collection of the Museum of Modern Art in New York City. An ingenious counterweight system and swivelling base allow for adjustment to any angle. Available as both a table lamp and as a floor lamp (shown) with the addition of a 27″-high base, Tizio stands 46½″ tall at its fullest extension and is finished in matte black. **6.** Ernesto Gismondi's Aton Fluorescent is offered in a choice of white, charcoal gray, black, or anodized aluminum finishes and in two heights, 65″ and 83½″. The larger takes a 58-watt fluorescent tube, the smaller a 36-watt tube; both are supplied by the manufacturer.

3

4

5

6

1

2

3

1. **IPI** distributes Beam, designed by Enrico Bona for Skipper. A halogen lamp with V-shaped extruded aluminum stem and adjustable reflector, it is available in black, red, white, or aluminum finish and in floor, wall, and ceiling models. **2.** Designed by Milleluci for **Illuminating Experiences**, these halogen lamps each stand 72″ tall and come in polished brass or lacquered black or white finish. **3. Classic Illumination** offers this graceful glass shade in a variety of colors. It is available as either a hanging or floor lamp and is 14″ in diameter. **4.** Designed by Veart for **Illuminating Experiences**, this 72″-high lamp comes in white or black. **5.** The Corona Lamp, designed by Lorenzo Porchelli, is offered by **The Museum of Modern Art**. It features a rice-paper shade atop a black metal frame, the whole 52½″ tall. **6.** Artisans Mickey and Roberta Ackerman of **Conversions** created this unusual anodized aluminum lamp with glass lenses. **7.** Truck, a halogen lamp designed by New Society for **Illuminating Experiences**, stands 75½″ tall at its full extension and tilts from the base while the etched glass diffuser stays level. **8.** Created by Piero Castiglioni of Fontana Arte for **Interna Designs**, the Edy halogen lamps are of green-gray varnished metal. **9.** Gregotti Associates designed the streamlined Segno Uno floor lamp for Fontana Arte. Distributed by **Interna Designs**, the 68″-tall fixture has a varnished metal base and opaline glass shade, both available in a variety of colors.

4

5

6

7

8

9

1

2

3

Among the most dramatic and original floor lamps offered by **Nessen Lamps** are those in its Luci of Italy collection. The entire Nessen line, however, includes a lighting device to appeal to every contemporary taste. **1.** Rete features an eye-catching, scalloped white glass shade with black stripes. The floor lamp, 72″ tall with a polished chrome base, takes a 150-watt bulb. The hanging lamp is 19″ in diameter. Matching table lamps are also offered. **2.** This swing-arm floor lamp, 31″ wide, is adjustable in height from 49″ to 60″, making it a most versatile piece. Fitted with a glass reflector and either a three-way bulb (maximum 150 watts) or a dimmer switch, it comes with a choice of linen or pleated shades. **3.** Adonis, designed by Gianfranco Frattini for Nessen/Luci, is 74″ of sleek aluminum column, its bulb recessed into a blown tempered glass diffuser. It's available in red, white, or black finish on a black base. **4.** The Alom/C floor lamp and matching wall fixture are made in five finishes: black, ivory matte, ruby, white, and polished brass. The ribbed shade takes a 300-watt halogen bulb. The floor lamp is 72″ tall, while the wall lamp is 14″ wide.

5. Tomo, designed by Toshyuki Kita for Nessen/Luci, sports a decorative red ball as a counterbalance for its unusual T-shaped arm. Arm and reflector rotate 180 degrees; color combinations are white/black or yellow/black with red. **6.** This floor/wall lamp duo is available in polished brass or chrome; the floor model, 70″ tall, features a foot dimmer switch for its 300-watt halogen bulb. **7.** Arco, aptly named for its graceful arched stem, is offered in polished brass or black finish. The reflector, taking a 300-watt halogen bulb, rotates; the whole is 81″ tall and 57″ wide.

4

5

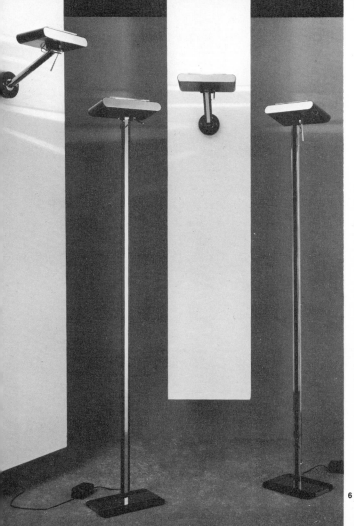

6

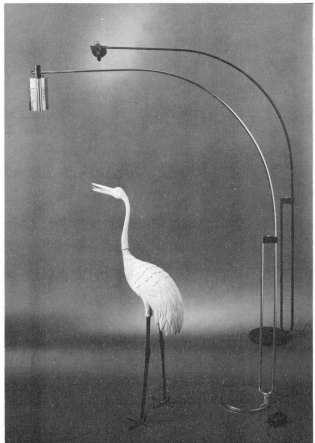

7

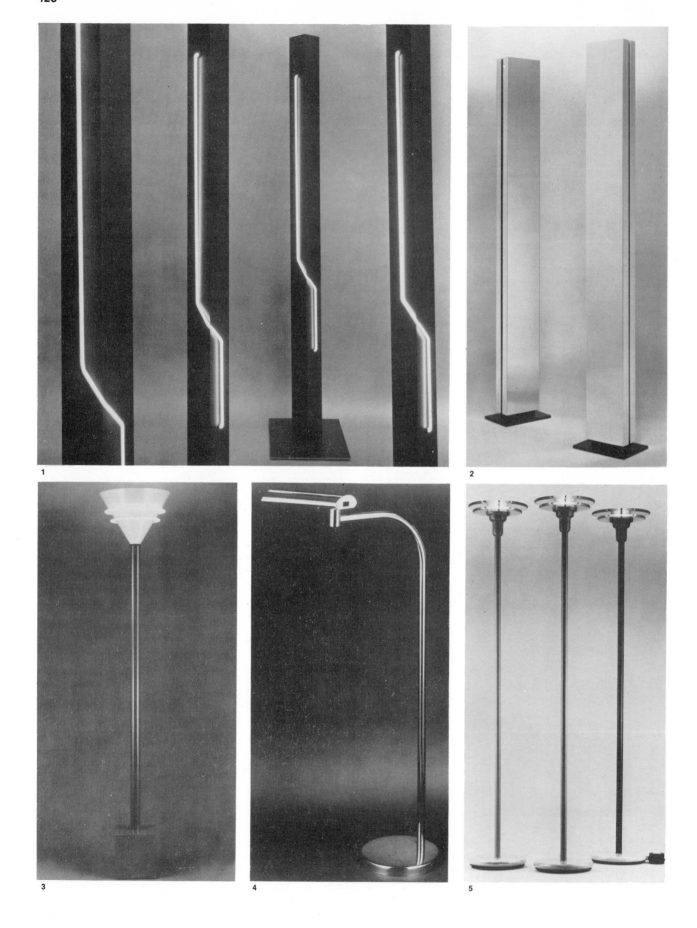

1

2

3

4

5

The name **George Kovacs** has been synonymous with the finest in lighting design for many years, as the examples shown on these pages will confirm. **1.** Designed by Dan Chelsea is a futuristic neon tube in blue, white, orchid or ruby red, which wraps two sides of a black aluminum square column, the whole 72″ tall. The column is fitted with a 400-watt halogen bulb. **2.** Just the touch of a finger will turn the 400-watt tungsten halogen bulb in this polished brass (or polished chrome) lamp on or off, or adjust it to one of three levels. Designed by David Winfield Willson, it is 74″ high. **3.** Not for the timid, Be Bop by Rudi Stern and Nils Eklund glows colorfully, with its yellow shade, blue stem, red base, and pink and blue neon rings. A work of art, it stands 71″ tall. **4.** The talented Robert Sonneman designed this sinuous polished chrome fixture, also available in polished brass. The shade rotates 350 degrees; the stem is 44″ high and extends from 15″ to 24″ in width. **5.** Sonneman also created this ultramodern 70″-tall fixture, topped by twin glass shades reflecting a 250-watt halogen bulb. The stem is available in black, gray, or pink on a marble base. **6.** Reminiscent of the pioneering designs of Charles Rennie Mackintosh and others of the early Arts and Crafts movement, Sonneman's multi-columned polished brass lamp has a dramatic black stem and base lit by a 400-watt halogen bulb. **7.** This Belgian-made torch with adjustable head comes in black, white, red, and yellow. It takes a 500-watt quartz halogen bulb and is fitted with a full-range dimmer. **8.** The Lamporghini, in black, red, or white, is available as a floor, desk, or clip-on lamp. Each takes a 50-watt reflector bulb.

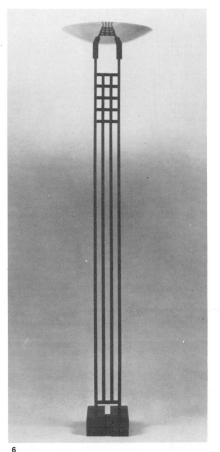

6

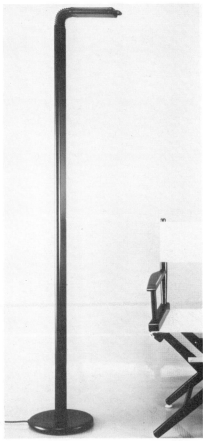

7

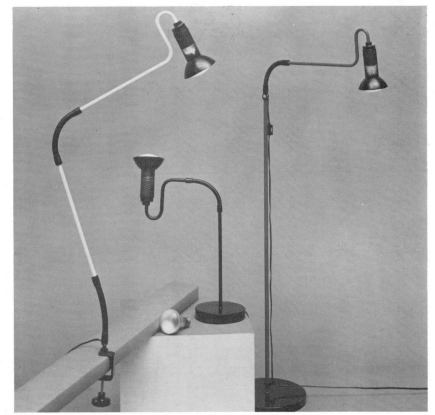

8

Presented here are four more representative examples of the fine work done by **George Kovacs** designers, whether working in traditional or startlingly futuristic modes. Each fixture shows the care and thought given to detail as well as to overall appearance. **1.** A black steel frame, 68″ in height, supports the white diffusing material of this ultramodern floor lamp designed by Dan Chelsea. Along with a 300-watt halogen bulb which provides sensible illumination, there is a whimsical surprise—a stretch of blue, red, or aqua neon to provide a touch of color. **2.** Classic in style, this trim fixture reaches a height of 54″. The contemporary touch is that base, stem, and 18″-diameter shade are all one color: choose from traditional black or white, or more daring taupe or plum. The three-way bulb lights to a maximum power of 250 watts. **3.** Admirers of minimalist styling will appreciate Peter Hamburger's simple, balanced design. Available in white or gray, this floor lamp is 66″ tall, with a shade just 8¾″ in diameter. The fixture accommodates a three-way bulb (350-watt maximum). **4.** Swing-arm styling is a great convenience and sometimes a necessity for proper illumination. But practicality doesn't have to be unattractive, as this handsome design proves. Choose a finish of polished brass or polished chrome and a shade of stretched natural muslin or beige linen. The floor model is 53″ tall and can be ordered with a brown vinyl stem with brass fittings. The table lamp is 24″ tall; the wall lamp extends to 21″. Each takes a three-way bulb with illumination up to 250 watts.

2

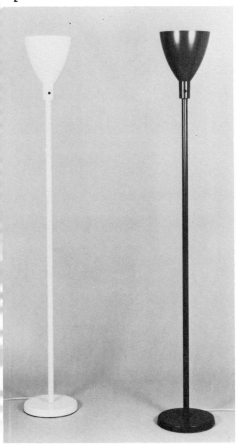

3

4

Koch & Lowy's superb design and workmanship is based on thirty years' experience. **1.** Flash-Lite comes in polished brass or chrome and in a wide range of models. The triple-shade floor lamp is 60″ tall; the single one 46″ tall (the swing-arm version extends from 34″ to 46″). **2.** Dynasty, 54″ high , has a white acrylic shade on a brass or chrome stem. Choose hanging and table models as well. **3.** Footsteps has legs of yellow enamel or black Nextel (a suede-like material). The shade comes in black Nextel or polished brass or chrome; the feet are gray Nextel. Lit by a 500-watt halogen bulb, the lamp is 74″ tall and 18″ wide at the base. **4.** Eagle, designed by Piotr Sierakowski, is a simple 72″ column with a 250-watt halogen bulb. Opt for polished brass or chrome, or gray or black Nextel. **5.** The Sphere Tree, 59″ high, comes in polished brass, chrome, or California brass. It takes three 75-watt bulbs. **6.** Order the Universal with black leather handle and black shaft accented by polished chrome, or with honey leather handle, brown shaft, and polished brass accents. It takes a 75-watt bulb; dimensions are 28″ by 58″. **7.** Delta is finished in black or gray Nextel. The 73″ fixture takes a 500-watt halogen bulb; the shade pivots 45 degrees. **8.** Dramatic is the word for Halogena: a hand-blown etched glass layered shade sits on a black support, upheld by a polished brass or chrome stem and base. The 500-watt halogen bulb is included. **9.** Spats is 69″ tall and takes a 150-watt halogen bulb. Its opal glass shade tops a stem finished in polished chrome, brass, white, or black. **10.** The unusual frosted glass shade of Ciloster arches over a black or red and gray stem, the whole 76″ high. A foot switch controls the 250-watt halogen bulb.

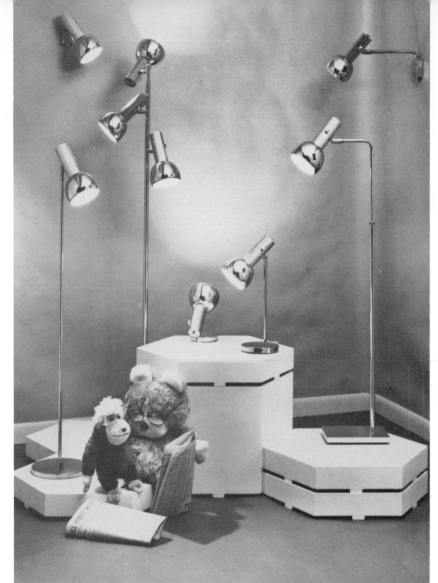

1

2

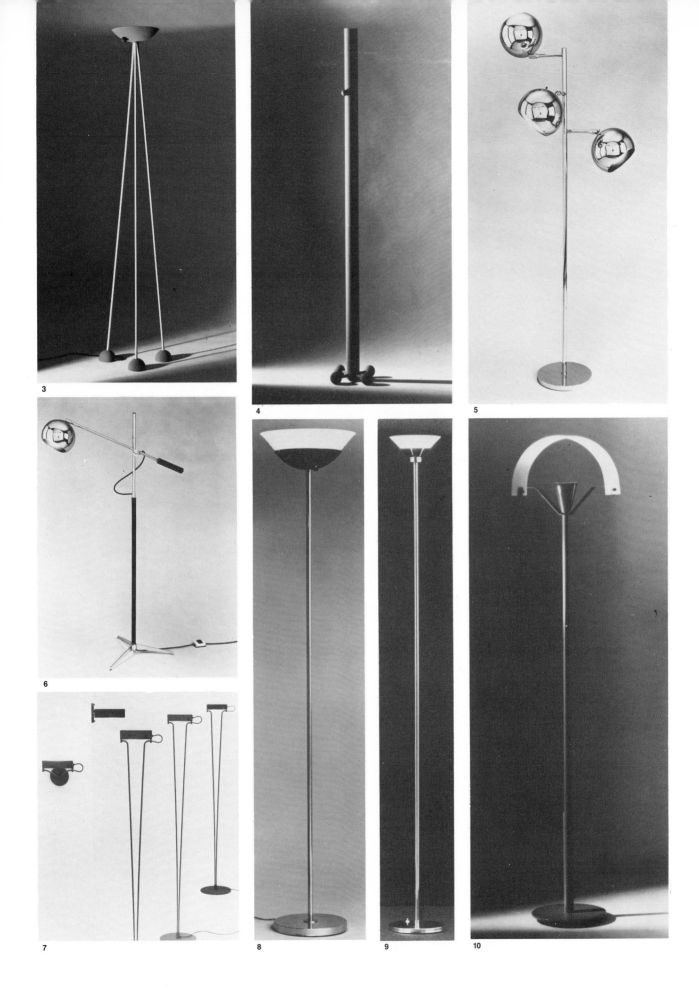

3

4

5

6

7

8

9

10

Modern Table Lamps

Whether used to enliven a dark corner or to illuminate close work such as reading or sewing, table lamps are a necessary addition to the furnishings of virtually any room. Selection of contemporary styles need not be limited to the customary shade-with-base varieties. Modern designers have created fantastic variations that are both superbly designed and functional. Lamps that swing, move along tracks, tilt up and down; lamps of fiberglas, chrome, brass, marble, crystal, and paper—all are available in a range of colors to suit every taste and complement every piece of furniture. In our age of design reinterpretation, the tradition of mechanical fixtures whose beauty derives from their purposefulness carries on in the technologically astounding table lamps now being made. Using halogen or fluorescent bulbs, lighting designers create streamlined fixtures with amazing brilliance.

Interna Designs offers a number of avant-garde table lamp designs sure to find favor among those of an adventurous spirit. As is the case with so many modern decorative pieces, these are all the creations of Italian artisans. **1.** The Scintilla Tavolo halogen lamp by Fontana Arte is made of anodized aluminum. Finishes available are gray or black, or it can be ordered with a base and shade of black and a stem lacquered in red, yellow, or blue. The lamp is 6½″ by 11¾″. **2.** Designed by Plana, Perielio is a halogen lamp with three articulated joints for great flexibility. Available in black or white, it stands 43″ tall. A floor model is also offered. **3.** Canna da Tavolo, created by Piero Castiglioni and Roberto Menghi for Fontana Arte, features a blown glazed glass shade on a metal base of light or dark gray or beige, the whole about 20″ tall. **4.** This adjustable halogen floodlight sits on a cylindrical base of yellow, red, or blue blown glass 7″ in diameter. Called Parodia, it is 14″ tall and was designed by Piero Castiglioni. **5.** An interesting modern rendition of the classic library lamp, called simply number 0836, was designed by Pietro Chiesa of Fontana Arte. It has a thick crystal base and white opaline shade supported by polished brass mounts and is roughly 9″ tall. **6.** The whimsically named Oz was designed by Daniela Puppa and Franco Raggi for Fontana Arte. Its thick crystal base supports a 12½″ cone of blown colored glass, available in gray, pink, or yellow. **7.** Fontana Arte designers Gae Aulenti and Piero Castiglioni created Parola, a halogen lamp with a clear glass stem and crystal base. The diffuser on this 20″-tall fixture is offered in pink, yellow, or blue glass.

1

2

3

4

5

6

7

Artemide's table lamps are no less dramatic or interesting than its floor fixtures, as the examples shown on these pages prove. As is true of so much modern design, many of the most unusual and original offerings are the work of Italian artists. **1.** No matter the color scheme of the room, Aggregato Stelo is available in a shade to complement it. Its conical shade, in white, red, green, or gray opaline or charcoal gray metal, is offered in both a 15″ and a 20½″ diameter and takes a 100-watt bulb. Designed by Enzo Mari and Giancarlo Fassina, it is 23″ tall. **2.** The Sintesi task lamp by Ernesto Gismondi has a utilitarian 35″ arm which stretches to a maximum of 40″ in height. Available in white, black, or beige, it takes a 75-watt bulb and can also be ordered in a clamp-on style or a smaller table model with an angular metal hinged base. **3.** Area 50 Curva's sinuous curved stem supports a free-form white shade which accommodates a 100-watt bulb. Its romantic styling is the work of Mario Bellini. **4.** Ernesto Gismondi designed Alistro, whose energy-saving fluorescent bulb sits on a utilitarian beige arm and sculptured base. The moveable arm takes up a maximum width of about 35″; the lamp is nearly 44″ tall. **5.** Pausania, though ultramodern in design, seems inspired by the classical Greek and Roman arch. Ettore Sottsass created the 18″ by 17″ fluorescent lamp in a black and green color combination. **6.** Sleek simplicity characterizes Dafne, designed by O. Halloween. Offered in white or in gray with a white shade, it takes a 100-watt bulb and is 14⅜″ tall.

1

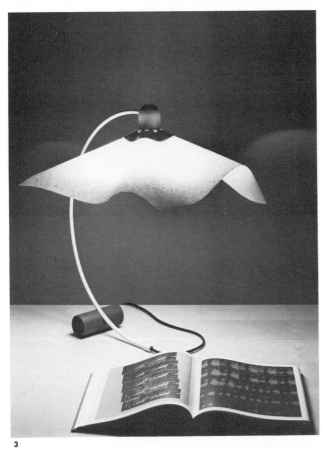

3

4

5

6

1

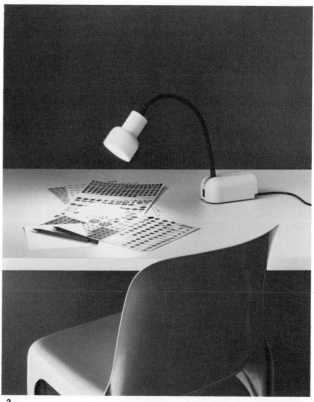

2

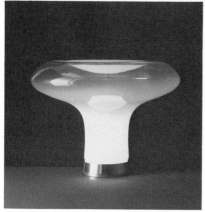

3

5

Several of the **Artemide** table lamps shown on this page are not only useful as lighting devices, but, properly placed, will give the effect of fine works of sculpture as well. **1.** Mezzachimera is such a piece. Designed by Vico Magistretti, its graceful curved white shade diffuses the light of three tubular 60-watt bulbs. Just 9½″ wide, it is 30½″ tall at its highest point. **2.** The flexible black stem of Ernesto Gismondi's Tholos Studio lamp connects a base and shade of white, black, yellow,

or China red. A standard 60-watt bulb is accommodated; maximum height is 22″. **3.** Lesbo's sensually shaped hand-blown glass diffuser conceals a 75-watt bulb. Designed by Angelo Mangiarotti, the mushroom-like lamp is 19¾″ wide by 14¾″ tall. **4.** Tizio, the most famous of Artemide's lighting designs, looks no less contemporary today than when it was created by Richard Sapper in 1971. Also available in a floor model (shown in the floor lamp section), it is an

angular stretch of matte black aluminum which adjusts to a maximum width of 37″ and a maximum height of 46½″. This classic style accommodates a 55-watt halogen bulb. **5.** One of Artemide's newest models, Eubea, designed by Alberto Fraser, features a gray thermoplastic and metal base and a cut-glass diffuser. The twin arms holding the shade are adjustable; maximum height is 14⁹⁄₁₆″. Two frosted tubular 60-watt bulbs provide ample illumination.

Among the most contemporary of **George Kovacs'** table lamps are the four shown below, any one of which would complement a stylish modern interior. **6.** Choose this high-style design by Robert Sonneman in either polished glass, brass, aluminum, and black enameled steel or polished glass with colorful red, yellow, and aqua fittings. The halogen lamp, Kovacs' model 6770, takes a 100-watt bulb and is equipped with a full-range dimmer. It is 17½″ by 15¼″. **7.** This sleek, minimal design by Stephen Diskin is available in floor, desk, and wall models. The floor and desk lamps are 42″ and 11″ high, respectively; the wall model extends 15″. Each is fitted with a 13-watt fluorescent bulb; colors available are black, white, lilac, and gray. **8.** Robert Sonneman designed Odyssey in black or white with chrome arms. The versatile fixture extends 13″ to 30″ from the center of the base; its height is adjustable from 6″ to 34″; and it rotates 360 degrees. The rectangular diffuser takes a 150-watt halogen bulb. **9.** A sleek column of polished brass encloses a 75-watt bulb in this design by Milo Baughman. The 15″-lamp is equipped with a full-range dimmer.

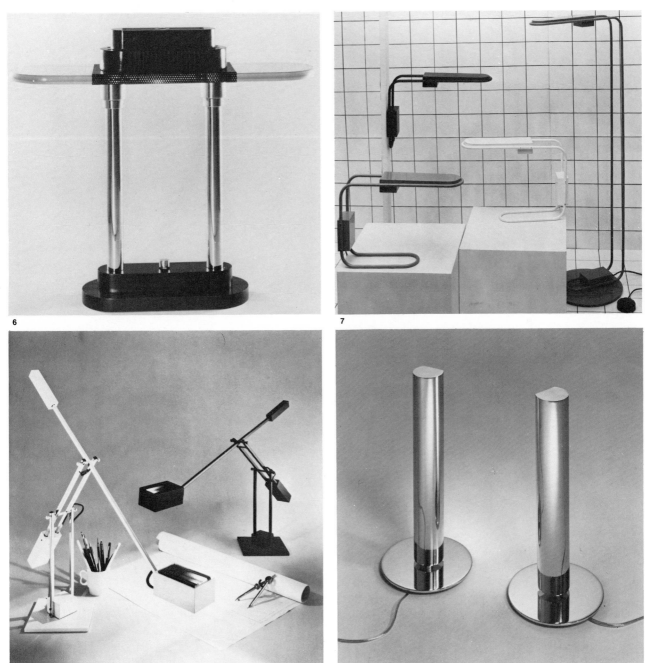

6

7

8

9

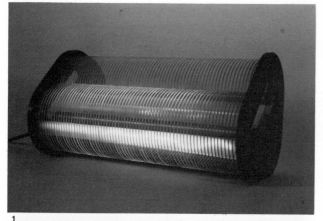

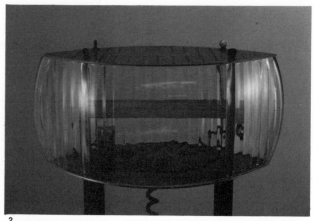

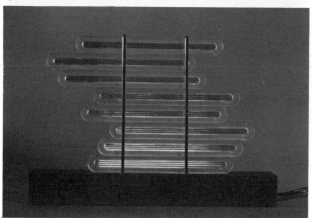

1

2

3

5

6

4

Some of the most unusual and adventurous designs in modern lighting are the work of individual craftsmen and artisans such as **Mickey and Roberta Ackerman** of **Conversions.** The table lamps shown here—lighting sculptures, really—are certain conversation pieces and deserving of careful placement in a setting which will show them to proper advantage. The Ackermans use a variety of materials in their collaborative efforts, materials which include both natural (wood) and man-made (microwave tubing) substances. **1.** Glass discs, anodized aluminum, and stainless steel comprise this avant-garde fixture. It is 13″ wide and 7″ high. **2.** Perhaps an early automobile headlamp was the inspiration for this spectacular fixture. **3.** Piled tubes of cast glass give this steel and aluminum lamp a fascinating sculptural effect. **4.** This pair of table lamps seems inspired by the simple candleholders of colonial days, yet their composition is anything but old-fashioned. Glass, copper, brass, and epoxy-coated steel are combined in these 21″-tall fixtures; the bases are 12″ wide. **5.** Appropriate for use either at a desk or on a side table, this piece is made of bent and machined aluca-bond, an architectural building material. **6.** Aluminum and glass are combined in this rectilinear fixture; its dimensions are 12″ by 4″ by 14″.

Examples of the unique contemporary designs of three other craftsmen are illustrated on this page. Each brings a distinctive style to the creation of lighting devices that are as much works of art as they are useful illumination for desk or table; all have had numerous gallery and museum exhibitions and are represented in both private and public collections. **7. Mark McDonnell** creates colorful hand-blown glass table lamps on painted wood bases and is particularly noted for the unusual patterns which decorate the glass. Both lamps shown are set on 8″-square bases; the taller is 22″ high. **8. Ray King**'s early interest in stained glass led to work with various forms of sculpture and to unusual lighting devices such as the Moon Lamp illustrated here. Optical etched glass tops a bronze and slate base in a fixture 13½″ by 6″ by 17½″. **9, 10. Hap Sakwa** works in wood and acrylic. Beacon has a lacquered, turned-wood base and a ⅛″ acrylic shade to diffuse the light of a 9-watt fluorescent bulb. Dimensions are 8½″ by 22″. Fountain, 13″ by 21″, is composed of the same materials and also accommodates a fluorescent bulb.

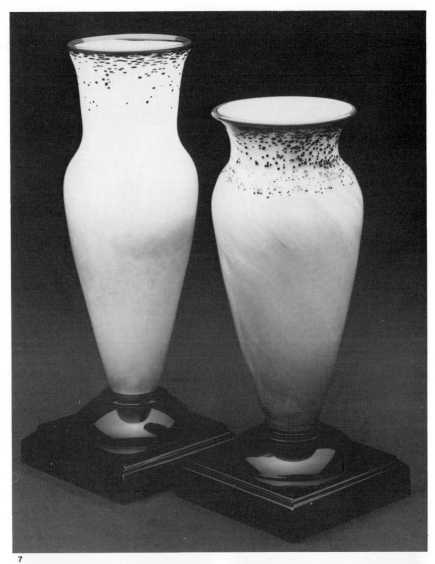

7

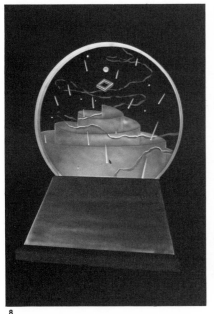

8

9

10

One of the reasons for the distinctive styling of most **Nessen** lighting fixtures is that the company collaborates with many top European designers to offer the best of their creations exclusively to American customers. Another can be found in the company's origins. Founded by Bauhaus devotee Walter von Nessen, who invented the swing-arm lamp, Nessen has continued to be interested in the most innovative and progressive designs. The superb fixtures on these two pages are typical of the firm's brilliance.
1. Kandido, one of Nessen/Luci's newest offerings, is among its most avant-garde in style. Created by F. A. Porsche, designer of the Porsche 904 and 911 Carrera sports cars, it features three antenna-like rods which connect the base and reflector. The rods swivel at both ends so that they can move in tandem or be positioned to rotate around each other. This flexibility allows the halogen bulb to be aimed in a number of directions. Finished in black and chrome, Kandido has a minimum height of 11″ and a maximum of 34″. **2.** It would be easy to think of a number of places where this energy-saving fluorescent table lamp would provide useful illumination. Small enough to fit in the most confined space (16″ by 16″), it is simply styled to blend with most modern furnishings. Available in baked enamel in red or black with polished brass or polished chrome accents, it can be specially ordered in a color to meet any individual preference.

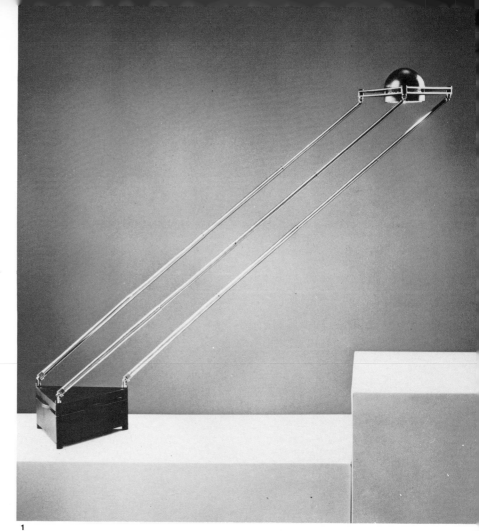

1

2

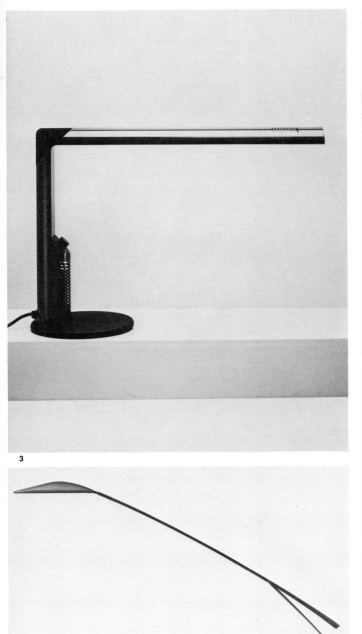

3

5

6

3. Abele, designed by Gianfranco Frattini, is an angular composition of aluminum painted white, black, red or gray on a black base. 22″ by 15″, it takes a 50-watt halogen bulb. **4.** Arnia's glass bases are offered in pink, straw, or white; the shantung shade, in black or white. Choose

two sizes: 23″ tall with a 20″-diameter shade, or 27½″ tall with a 23″ shade. **5.** Designed by Mario Barbaglia and Marco Colombus for Nessen/Paf, Dove is aptly named for its graceful, sweeping lines. The halogen lamp is practical as well; arm and reflector

move up and down, and can be rotated around the base. **6.** Offered in two sizes, 20″ tall with a 12½″-diameter shade or 23″ with a 19″ shade, Bucaneve Ventaglio has shades of blown glass, and fittings of polished brass.

2

3

1

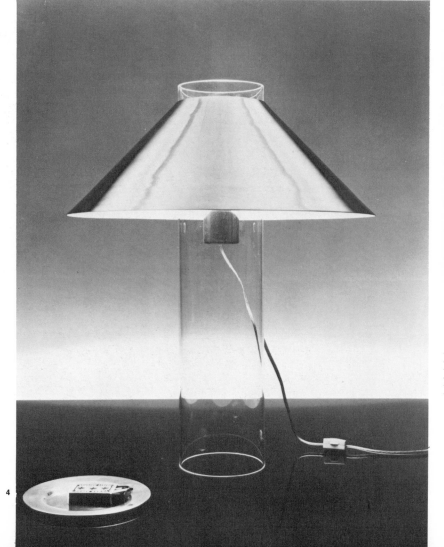

5

4

1. The smaller of the two table lamps pictured here, called the Eyeball Spotlight, was designed by Pat Hoffman for **Koch & Lowy.** Of polished brass or chrome and plexiglass, it measures 7½″ by 10″.

2. Koch & Lowy calls this 12″ by 10″ lamp Wings. It features a frosted glass shade and a base of green, burgundy, yellow, or jade enamel; it can also be ordered in Nextel, a suede-like material, in black or gray. **3.** Delta, an energy-efficient fluorescent lamp from **Koch & Lowy,** is available in a variety of models—from floor lamp to pin-up —in addition to the table lamp shown here. It measures 20″ by 14″ and comes in gray or black Nextel. **4.** Classic styling is interpreted in a novel way in this Glasslight from **Koch & Lowy.** It comes with a clear glass or white opaque glass base and a choice of polished brass, polished chrome, or pleated linen shade and stands 22″ tall. **5.** The Sculpture table lamp by **Koch & Lowy** is 14½″ by 20″ of hand-blown opaque white glass which takes a 150-watt bulb. **6. Illuminating Experience's** line of Murano table lamps is offered in two sizes; the fixtures range in height from 9½″ to 26″. Each is a one-piece form of hand-blown opaque glass and accommodates a 75-watt bulb. **7.** This is one of many dramatic and original designs available through architects and designers who feature **Karl Springer** furnishings. The sleek modern fixture is made of lucite and metal. **8.** Kamsah is an uncompromisingly geometric design from **Illuminating Experiences.** The ultramodern fixture measures 21½″ by 14½″ and accommodates a halogen bulb. **9.** Hand-blown Venetian glass in the shapes or spheres, cylinders, and flasks makes for unusual accent lighting from **Paul Hanson.** Heights range from 9¼″ to 12″. **10.** Designed by Hans von Klier for Skipper, the Concorde is distributed by **Innovative Products for Interiors.** As sleek as the supersonic transport for which it is named, the aluminum halogen lamp has a fully adjustable arm.

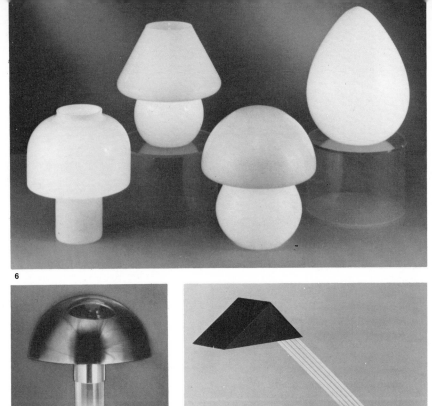

6

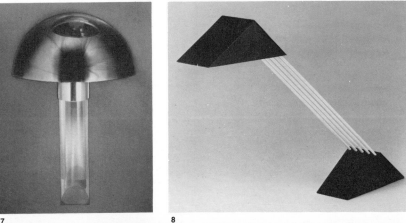

7

8

9

10

Modern Wall Fixtures

Lights intended to be hung from the walls can conserve precious space on desk or table, offer security and convenience in a dark hallway or over the bed, or highlight striking architectural features of a room. Whether used singly, in pairs, or in groups; whether the light source is fixed or moveable, hung from an armature or affixed directly to the wall—such lights can be an integral part of a room's design scheme and often enhance pictures placed nearby.

2

Dramatic European styling is the hallmark of **Artemide**'s offerings in wall fixtures, as well as in the floor and table lamps pictured elsewhere in this book. **1.** Mario Bellini interprets Area 50 in both wall and ceiling models. The sconce projects 19¼″ and is offered in three sizes, from 7⅞″ to 19⅝″ in diameter. **2.** Sanded glass gracefully diffuses the light of Angelo Mangiarotti's Egisto, available in wall and corner wall models. **3.** Clipeo, by Eric Gottein, is designed in gray and white painted metal. Its 13″ width accommodates two 100-watt bulbs. **4.** Icaro is a gray metal and cut crystal flight of fancy by Carlo Forcolini which takes a 150-watt halogen bulb. **5.** Solid brass and hand-blown opaline glass are the components of Commodore by Ernesto Gismondi. It projects 10¼″ from the wall and is 11″ tall. **6.** Örni Halloween's Gea measures a mere 6¹⁹⁄₆₄″ in diameter. Offered in white, black, China red, or gray, it can be grouped to interesting effect. **7.** A simple half-sphere gets a new interpretation in Doral by Ernesto Gismondi. Of brass and hand-

1

blown glass, it is available in two sizes, 11″ by 6¾″ and 13½″ by 8¾″. **8.** Gismondi envisioned Giasole as a sweep of sanded glass. Dimensions are 11″ by 4²¹⁄₆₄″. **9.** The diffusor and the bulb are one in Gismondi's Biltmore. Offered in two sizes, the brass fixture is supplied with a pearl white 60- or 100-watt decorative bulb. **10.** Cyclos deserves a spacious wall to set off its generous girth (15¾″ in diameter). Designed by Michele de Lucchi, it is gray with a white diffusor.

3

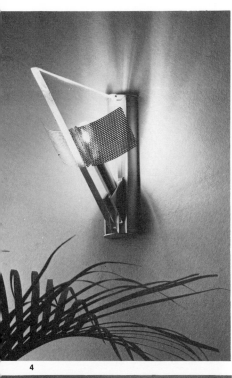

4

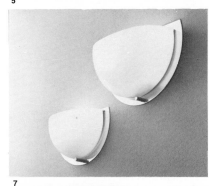

5

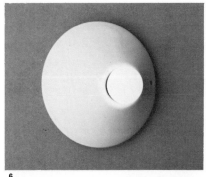

6

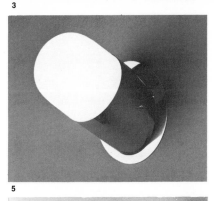

7

8

9

10

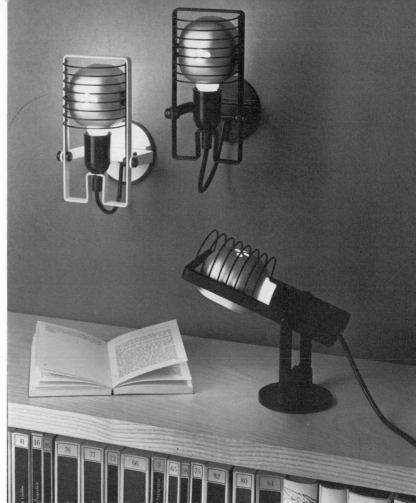

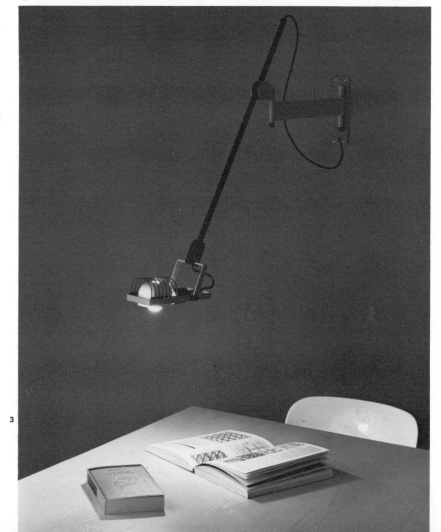

1. Vico Magistretti created **Artemide**'s Mania (9½″ high) and Grand Mania (11″ high) sconces. The classic ovoid shapes are available in white or opaline glass and each accommodates a standard bulb. **2.** The Sintesi spotlight designed by Ernesto Gismondi for **Artemide** can be wall-mounted or used as a table lamp. Available in white, black, or red, it measures 4″ by 10½″ and takes a standard 75-watt bulb. **3.** Gismondi's Sintesi arm lamp extends a maximum of 47″ from the wall, offering great flexibility of placement. **Artemide** offers it in white, black, and red.

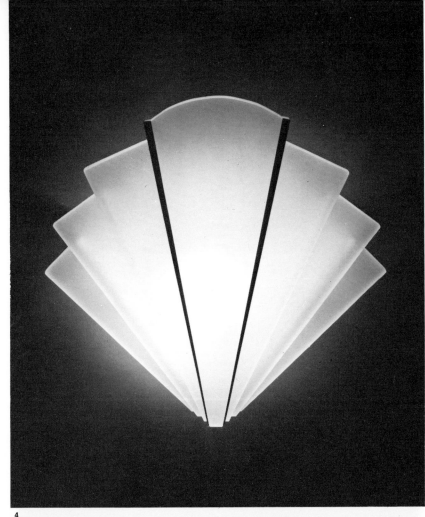

4

Three examples of the creative uses of acrylic as interpreted by **Plexability**, a master of the medium for more than two decades, are shown here. These are all from the company's line of Lumia sconces designed by Michael Zevy Berkowitz. While the dimensions of the models shown are given, Plexability can make these designs in a size to meet any individual specifications and welcomes custom commissions as well. **4.** The classic fan shape has been adapted as a design of wall sconces for centuries. This modern version is frosted acrylic accented with mirrored strips. It is 18″ wide, 16″ tall, and 8″ deep. **5.** Frosted acrylic wedges are outlined in black for a dramatic sculptural effect in a sconce that appears to be cantilevered from the wall. This Plexability design measures 12″ by 11″ and projects 8″ from the wall. **6.** Gently curved frosted acrylic diffuses the light of a 25-watt to 100-watt bulb. This modern sconce may be composed of space-aged material, but it has a romantic, timeless feel about it. The model shown is 12″ by 16″ and has a depth of 8″.

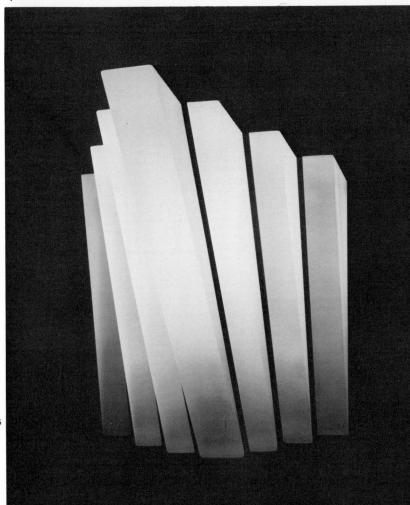

5

6

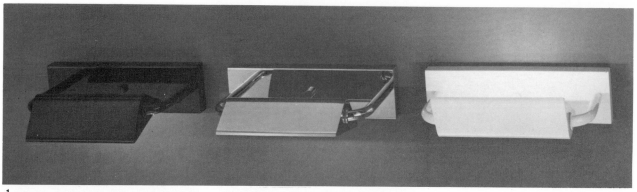

1

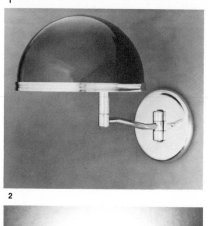

2

4

3

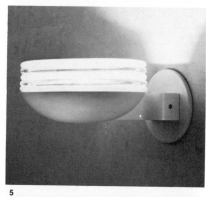

5

6

The thirteen different wall sconces shown on these two pages are the work of six different lighting companies and two talented craftsmen with no corporate affiliation; taken together they give some indication of the wide variety of modern wall lighting available today. **1.** Designed by Milleluci for **Illuminating Experiences**, these geometric brackets can be ordered in polished brass or lacquered black or white. Each is 11½″ by 3¼″ and takes a 300-watt halogen bulb. **2, 3.** Green, cognac, white, or satin-finish glass trimmed with brass composes the classic Ring from **Illuminating Experiences**. Magia, from the same source, is a sleekly molded sweep of solid brass 12½″ by 9¾″ which is available in several finishes. It takes a 500-watt halogen bulb. **4, 5.** Designed by Roberto Pamio and Renato Toso for Leucos, Ventilla I and Aurora are exclusively available through **Innovative Products for Interiors**. Ventilla I features a ribbed white glass diffuser with baked enamel accents that can be ordered in several colors. Aurora sports a multicolored glass diffuser and baked enamel bowl-shaped reflector. **6. Classic Illumination**'s crystal half-cone shade accented with lacquered brass or chrome would look well in a variety of settings. Its dimensions are 8⅛″ by 8⅛″. **7.** Robert Sonneman designed this sleek wall torchiere for **George Kovacs**. A 200-watt halogen bulb with full-

7

8

9

range dimmer directs light upwards from the black and chrome fixture, which measures 16″ by 4½″. **8. Koch & Lowy**'s Spats is a halogen lamp which features an opal glass shade with chrome, white, or black accents. Its small size (5¾″ tall) makes it ideal for cramped, hard-to-illuminate spaces. **9.** The classic shell is interpreted in white satin glass in this pretty pin-up from **Koch & Lowy.** It's available in three sizes, ranging from 7″ to 10¼″ in width. **10, 11.** Among the many modern fixtures offered by **Progress Lighting** are these two simply designed wall sconces. The triple unit is 16″ tall and each shade takes two 60-watt bulbs which direct light both upward and downward. The single cylinder is available in white, black, or bronze and is 18″ in height. It accommodates two 150-watt bulbs. **12. Ray King** has molded colored aluminum into a striking modern sconce with a perforated screen. Its dimensions are 12″ by 18″; the projection is 14″. **13. Mark McDonnell**'s blue and black glass and marble sconce needs a large expanse of wall to display it properly: it is 15″ by 43″.

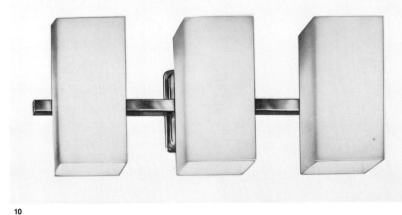

10

11

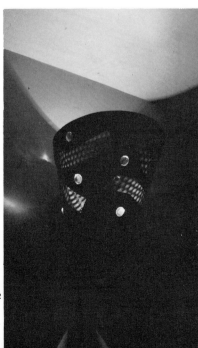

12

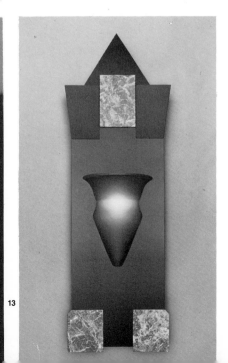

13

Modern Hanging and Ceiling Fixtures

Dominated for some time by an oligarchy of conically and spherically shaped lamps, hanging fixtures now incorporate new and neglected designs worth noting. Chandeliers, for example, are finding a new look, and fluorescent and halogen lighting now serve the demands of hanging lamps with originality and brilliance. Ceiling fixtures, too, though long the stepchildren of designers, boast a new versatility miles apart from the boring pillboxes of most lighting catalogues.

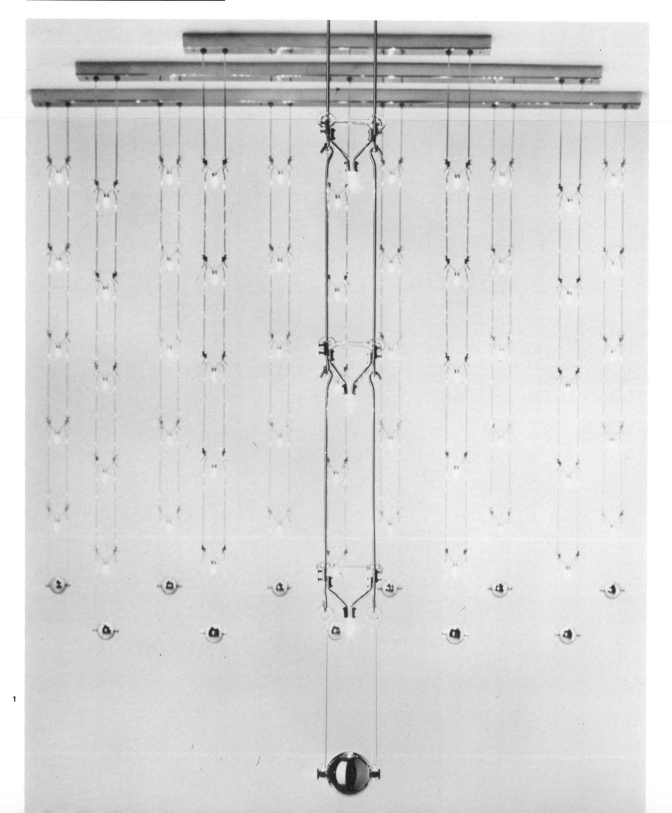

1

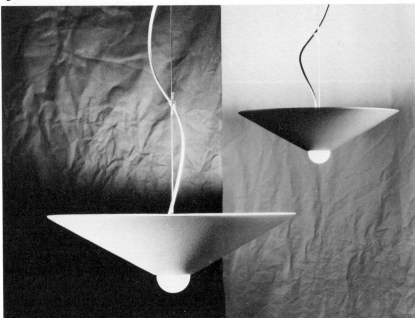

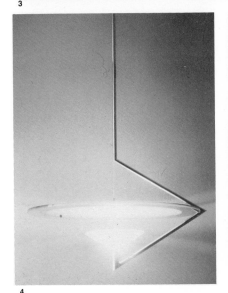

Interna Designs represents some of the most innovative lighting designers from the United States and Europe. Two cases in point are Italy's Fontana Arte and Lazin Lighting of New York, both of whose hanging lamps are represented on these pages. **1.** The basic component of Scintilla is the five-light vertical extension with chrome sphere shown in the forefront of this picture. Designed by Livio and Piero Castiglioni of Fontana Arte, it is meant to be combined in a variety of ways to create a chandelier-like effect of sparkling halogen bulbs. **2.** Designed by Larry Lazin of Lazin Lighting, Chelsea is a classic pendant that features a gray or white textured aluminum shade topped by a ring of red or white etched glass. Two sizes (14"- and 22"-diameter) are available; custom colors can be specified to blend with any decor. **3.** Makinaw, also a Lazin Lighting design, uses a 3" sand-etched glass dome to diffuse the light of two 100-watt bulbs. The 22"-diameter aluminum fixture comes in charcoal or white baked enamel or brushed aluminum finish; custom colors may be specified if desired. **4.** The dramatic Olampia from Fontana Arte can be varied in total length from 49½" to 73" by the addition of one or two extra segments of chrome-plated tubing. A white opal glass shade and sand-blasted crystal glass disk diffuse the powerful light of a halogen bulb. **5.** Clear or sand-blasted crystal disks surround a central crystal cylinder in Gio Ponti, another Fontana Arte creation. Accents are chrome-plated brass; the 21"-diameter fixture accommodates three 60-watt bulbs for more than adequate illumination.

1

2

3

4

5

6

7

8

9

Some of **Artemide**'s most exciting Italian designs can be ordered in various models to suit every lighting need. Many of the hanging lamps on these two pages, therefore, are represented elsewhere in other incarnations. **1.** The Aton halogen, designed by Ernesto Gismondi, can be depended from the ceiling or affixed to a wall. It comes in white, black, and red. **2.** Alesia, by Carlo Forcolini, adjusts in height from 43″ to 82″. It comes in white, black, or multicolor. **3.** The Sintesi suspension model by Ernesto Gismondi is 78¾″ high and takes a 75-watt bulb. Order it in white, black, or red. **4.** Nearly 32″ in diameter, the shade of Macumba 117 by Ö. Halloween is nickel-plated steel, protecting a 300-watt halogen bulb. **5.** Abolla, from CP & PR Associates, is a beige halogen lamp adjustable to a maximum of 155″ in height. **6.** Shown here with a charcoal gray cone, Aggregato by Enzo Mari and Giancarlo Fassina also comes in white, or with a glass sphere replacing the cone. **7.** Angelo Mangiarotti's Egina has a ribbed sanded glass shade which diffuses the light of a 100-watt bulb. **8.** Sidone can be adjusted from 29½″ to 53″ in length. The gray fixture, designed by De Pas—D'Urbino Lomazzi, takes a 500-watt halogen bulb. **9.** Maria Bellini's Area 50 can be had with or without counterweight. **10.** Shining stainless steel with a glass diffuser, Mera is a halogen lamp designed by Mario Marenco. **11.** Gray-painted metal surrounds a cut-glass diffuser in Michele De Lucchi's Cyclos. It accommodates two 100-watt bulbs and can be adjusted to a maximum height of 67″.

10

11

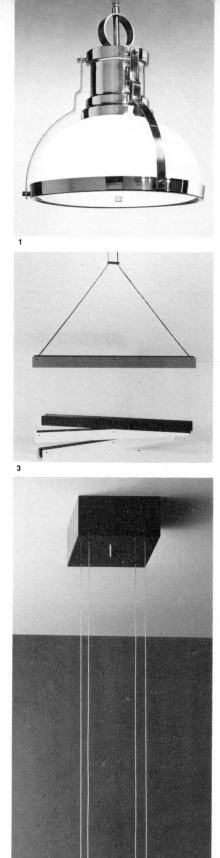

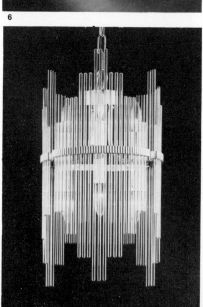

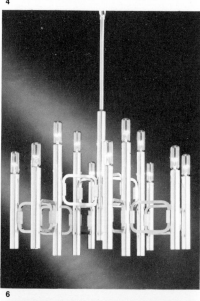

1. A combination of white glass, solid brass, and polished aluminum has been utilized in this David Winfield Willson design for **George Kovacs.** A Plexiglas diffuser softens the light from two 60-watt bulbs; the lamp is 14¼″ in diameter and 17″ high. **2. Progress Lighting**'s simple metal shade with reflective white interior is offered in gray, white, beige, or polished brass finish. The fixture itself is 16″ in diameter and 8¼″ tall; its total length is adjustable to a maximum of 48″. **3.** Noted designer Robert Sonneman created this angular steel and aluminum suspension lamp for **George Kovacs.** A 3″ fluorescent bulb (included) is fitted into the 40″ rectangular reflector, which can be ordered in white, black, red, or yellow with black fittings. **4. Metropolitan Lighting** uses frosted hand-blown glass with amber decoration for this classic bell. 16″ in diameter, it takes a 150-watt bulb. **5.** Designed by Ettore Sottsass, Jr., for Skipper and available exclusively from **Innovative Products for Interiors,** Hikary is a geometric halogen lamp of baked enamel. The squared-off reflector is suspended via four cables from a ceiling box which mirrors its shape and can attain a maximum length of 36″. **6.** Aldo Marchetti, who designed Modulo for **Illuminating Experiences,** seems to have taken an early colonial candelabrum as his inspiration and given it a very modern twist. Composed of polished and satin-finished brass, it accommodates

9

11

special bulbs which are included with the fixture. 23″ in diameter and 19″ high, it has an overall length of 54″. **7.** Clear crystal rods are arranged in modular shields on cast polished brass mountings in Diadem, available from **Illuminating Experiences.** Sciolari of Rome designed the fixture in three sizes, ranging from 9″ to 23″ in diameter. **8.** Fausto dalle Torre created Heirloom for **Illuminating Experiences.** Order it in polished brass or in a more weathered brass finish called "vintage." **9.** If space is at a premium, you might want to use only one of **Koch & Lowy**'s Bubble Pendants. Designed by Pat Hoffman, each is a mere 2″ in diameter and 5″ high, and is supplied with a 5″-diameter decorative bulb. **10.** Clear Venetian crystal with silver fittings sparkles in the Brunito Chandelier by **Koch & Lowy.** Also available in mixed amber and clear crystal, it is 21″ in diameter; a 12″ size is available by special order. **11.** Swirl is offered by **Koch & Lowy** in clear crystal with polished chrome or polished brass finish. It accommodates a 150-watt bulb and is 10½″ in diameter.

Even in the most spacious contemporary homes there are areas where the suspended ceiling fixtures shown on the previous pages would be inappropriate. In small hallways, bathrooms, and vestibules, a more compact form of lighting might be a better option. But as these **Artemide** designs prove, such a choice doesn't have to be mundane or ordinary. **1.** Offered in white, black, red, or green, Teti, a Vico Magistretti design, is less than 6″ in diameter and takes a 40-watt bulb. Several can be clustered for an unusual and dramatic effect. **2.** Luciano Vistosi's Onfale accommodates three 40-watt bulbs within its hand-blown glass diffuser. Also made in a wall model, it is 14″ in diameter. **3.** Ernesto Gismondi visualized Astoria in a choice of two sculpted glass forms, each of which depends about 12″ from a

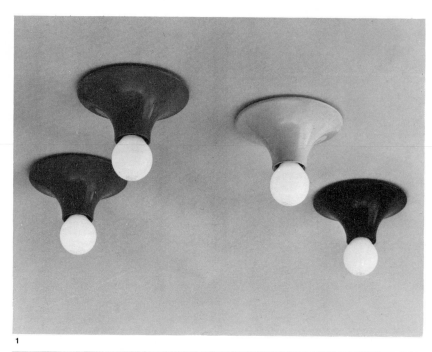

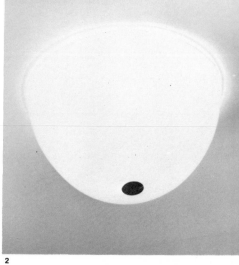

6

7

8

brass ceiling plate. **4.** Gismondi's Plaza is also made of hand-blown glass and is affixed to a brass plate. Placed on either ceiling or wall, it measures 13″ in diameter and can accommodate a 100-watt bulb. **5.** A conical hand-blown glass diffuser is the focal point of Faretra, designed by DePas, D'Urbino, Lomazzi. Roughly 8″ tall, it depends from a chrome and glass plate and takes a 150-watt halogen bulb. **6.** Angelo Mangiarotti's Egina, offered in 11″ and 15″ sizes, would look equally well on wall or ceiling. **7.** Choose Triteti in white, black, red, or green. Roughly 12″ in diameter, Vico Magistretti's design accommodates three 40-watt bulbs. Like its companion, Teti, shown on the opposite page, it seems to have been inspired by a common screw-base fixture; the result is anything but pedestrian, however. **8.** The molded shape of the Megaron ceiling fixture designed by Gianfranco Frattini seems to be a part of the room's architecture rather than an addition to it. When grouped as shown here, the result can be extremely effective. Order this lacquered aluminum halogen lamp in white, black, red, or green.

Track Lighting and Spotlights

Not so long ago, track lighting was thought to be the very latest form of illumination for the modern home. Although that is no longer the case (and in fact such systems have been overused to the point of cliché), there is no doubt that there are occasions when track lights are a valid choice. Because they can be aimed directly at a favorite painting, wall hanging, plant, or piece of sculpture without disrupting the overall design of the room and can create a specific mood or ambience, they can be very useful. All of the track lighting systems (and table spots) shown here will perform those functions. But they have been chosen with style in mind as well, proof that such a method of illumination doesn't have to be ill-designed or unattractive.

1. Progress Lighting offers a number of different styles of track lights, but probably none would be more practical than the six diminutive ones shown here. Available in polished brass, chrome, white, or black finishes, none is much larger than 4″ or 5″ in length. All can therefore be chosen with impunity to illumine hard-to-reach work areas under shelves or to provide accent lighting in a low-ceilinged room without distracting the eye from the focal point meant to be accentuated. **2.** This cylindrical track light from **Progress Lighting** features a built-in transformer. Offered in black,

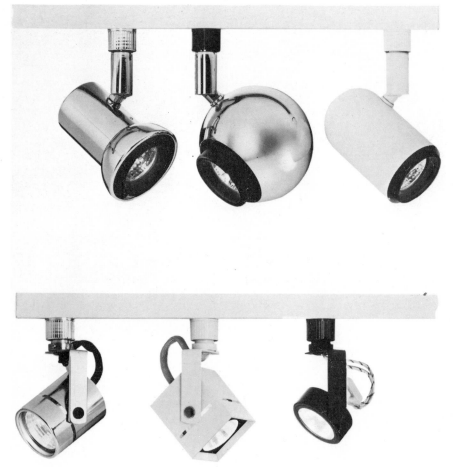

1

2

3

4

6

5

polished brass, or white finish, it is 6½″ tall and 3″ wide and can be positioned to concentrate its light beam in any number of directions. **3, 4.** The Italian artisans who create **Artemide**'s designs offer fixtures that are anything but ordinary; their track lighting is no exception. Ernesto Gismondi's Sintesi (*opposite page*) and Aton track lights are conversation pieces in themselves and definitely not just practical methods of illumination. Each is available in a choice of white, black, or red finish. The high-tech Sintesi measures 8⅜″ wide by 12″ high and takes a powerful 175-watt bulb. Aton takes an even brighter 300-watt halogen bulb and measures roughly 10″ by 8″. **5. George Kovacs'** rotund Spot comes in 5″- and 6″-diameter models which take 50- and 75-watt bulbs, respectively. Finished in black or white on a black tripod, they adjust to any position, and their small size makes them practical and unobtrusive choices for cramped spaces. **6.** One of **Artemide**'s newest offerings is Pilade, a series of low- and regular-voltage spot lamps offering a wide variety of models and optional accessories. Designed by Ernesto Gismondi, the lamp shown is available in blue, magenta, yellow, and gray finishes and takes a 50-watt halogen bulb. The die-cast aluminum fixture measures roughly 6″ by 7″.

Modern Outdoor Lighting

As is evident from the selections shown on the preceeding pages, owners of contemporary homes have many options when it comes to choosing well-designed and executed interior light fixtures. The reverse can be true, however, when it comes to outdoor lighting. The ubiquitous carriage lamp and its lantern spinoffs may be utilitarian, but they have no place on or near an ultramodern dwelling. Presented here are a number of alternatives much better suited to contemporary domestic architecture and its environs. Choose the right one to illuminate the front walk or driveway, highlight landscaping, or outline the garden path.

1

3

2

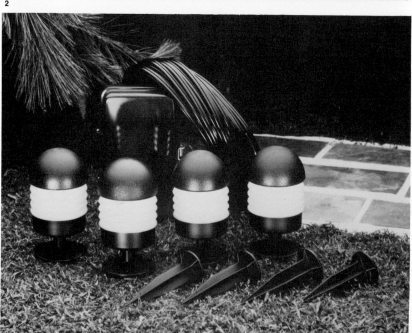

4

1. Tiered aluminum path and driveway lights from **Progress Lighting** include clear glass liners; each accommodates a 100-watt bulb. Finished in black, aluminum, or green, they measure 10″ in diameter and 9½″ in height. Install them permanently if desired, or keep them on hand for occasional evening entertaining. **2.** These forest-green lampholders from **Progress Lighting** come in sets of six. The bulbs are included, as are six colored lenses—two each in blue and green, one orange, and one red—to vary their effect. The ground spikes, cable, and control box with transformer and timer also come with each set. **3.** This unadorned bronze two-sided walk, driveway, or step light can be adjusted to a maximum height of 36″. The diffusers protect a 100-watt bulb and the fixture itself measures 5¼″ each side and 12¼″ high. **Progress Lighting** offers complementary styles as well. **4. Progress Lighting** packages these low-voltage black ground lights in sets of four. Each set includes 100 feet of cable, control box with timer and transformer, four lamps, and four ground spikes. Each lamp takes a 12-volt, high-intensity bulb. Up to four additional lights can be added to the set. **5.** Cerbero's dramatic styling is unmistakeably Italian in origin. English-green in color, Angelo Mangiarotti's design for **Artemide** is 15¾″ wide and can be ordered in 59″ or 98⅜″ heights. It takes one 100-watt bulb.

5

1

2

3

4

Whether your contemporary outdoor lighting needs include ceiling fixtures, lamps to flank the front door, or illumination for a path, walk, or driveway, the designers at **Artemide** have probably created a style that will suit admirably. **1.** Orca Virtuosa is offered in two heights, 35½″ and 49¼″, making it suitable both for patio or walk and driveway illumination. Designed by Ö. Halloween, it is 21″ in diameter. (You supply the ivy, of course.) **2.** Ernesto Gismondi's streamlined Tirso is a mere 2¾″ wide and can be ordered in 29¾″ or 50″ lengths. The post is anodized aluminum; the diffuser takes an energy-saving halogen bulb. **3.** Roughly 6″ in diameter, Aglaia comes in charcoal gray and accommodates a 75-watt bulb. Choose 23″ or 30″ heights. **4.** Imagine placing several of Sergio Mazza's Catilinas along a walkway, or positioning them at the edges of a patio. The charcoal-gray fixture takes a 75-watt bulb; its dimensions are 10″ by 12¾″. **5.** Edipo wall fixtures would look equally well grouped on a porch or framing an entranceway. Ö. Halloween's design comes in black or white, takes a 75-watt bulb, and measures 7⅞″ by 5¼″. **6.** Similar in concept is Halloween's Pafo. Also offered in white or black, it takes a 60-watt bulb and is small enough (7″ by 3¼″) to permit grouping in any number of arrangements for a dramatic effect. **7.** Sergio Mazza's Illo is the ceiling version of Catilina. Its base is charcoal gray; the diffuser takes a 75-watt bulb. **8.** Angelo Mangiarotti styled Cavea and Cavedio as the ceiling and wall versions, respectively, of his Cerbero post light. Each accommodates a 100-watt bulb. The ceiling fixture is 9″ high; the wall model, 14³⁄₁₆″ by 10⅜″.

5

6

7

8

Specialties

Whether your taste runs to modern or period spaces, at one time or another you will need the services of a supplier of lighting specialties. The modernist, for example, might find the task of finding a contemporary picture light an impossibility when most stores stock only the standard conservative model that has been around for the past half century or so. And the antiquarian, unless he has a very good electrical supply outlet in his neighborhood, is unlikely to find a reproduction carbon-filament bulb (c. 1909) at the local supermarket. Herewith, some of the wonders of today's enlightened lighting suppliers.

1. Any child would probably love one of these whimsical lamps from **George Kovacs.** Available in either a table model, as shown, or as a clamp-on, floor, or wall fixture, the ceramic head is styled as a teddy bear, panda, or goose. The maximum extension on the table lamp is 22″; it takes a standard 60-watt bulb. **2. Progress Lighting** offers these dressing-table or vanity lights in either polished chrome or polished brass finish; they can be fitted with either clear or frosted bulbs. Both five-light and three-light strips are available and the fixtures extend a mere 5″ from the wall. **3.** If you

1

2

3

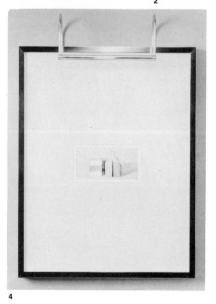

4

5

need illumination in a rustic vacation cabin or an outbuilding, but don't want to go to the expense of wiring the structure for electricity or bringing in a gas line, **Humphrey Products** can supply an innovative alternative to the kerosene lamp. Humphrey's Opalite operates on standard liquid propane gas. The fixture shown can be used either on a wall or a ceiling (the hanging lamp can be fitted with up to three lights). Each light provides the illumination of a 60-watt bulb. The enamel finish is offered in a choice of gray, copper, or gold tones; the

diffuser is glass. **4. Nessen Lamps** has introduced a solid-brass picture light which is the first to look as good as the picture it illuminates. Designed by Horst Lettenmayer, the Arcus is a sleek horizontal tube, suspended on curved arms. It houses a slender incandescent bulb. Available in three lengths ranging from 10″ to 34½″, it is offered in polished brass, polished chrome, bronze, or black or white baked enamel finishes. **5.** Designed by Ernesto Gismondi, **Artemide**'s Aton Mirror light is a slender strip of anodized aluminum available in

white, black, red, or natural finish. Its dimensions are roughly 4½″ by 30″. **6, 7. Lightworks** specializes in decorative lighting systems for large architectural spaces such as theatres, auditoriums, and restaurants. But its Tubelite system is flexible enough to be used in a contemporary home, as these examples show. The Tubelite strips come in any length up to a maximum of 24′. They can be arranged to form a chandelier, used to accent architectural details, hung as room dividers —the applications are limited only by your imagination.

6

7

1

1. Whether you need a replacement finial for an Art Deco table lamp or shades for a treasured gasolier, chances are you'll find them at the **Old Lamplighter Shop.** If you have an antique fixture that needs repair, the shop can handle it, even if it's a Tiffany look-alike that's missing a few bent glass panels. Old Lamplighter prides itself on its vast array of lamps and lamp parts; the company even has artists available to paint china shades to special order to match an existing base. **2.** Although both safety and practicality mitigate against using candles as a *permanent* source of light in even the most authentic of Colonial chandeliers, there is no need to settle for a cheap plastic substitute. **Elcanco**'s Morelite electric wax candle is handcrafted and hand-dipped with beeswax; it accommodates regular candelabra bulbs (which the company can also supply). The candle can be installed in an existing fixture or used alone, as shown here. Elcanco's other offerings include the Starlite electric wax candle, which is fitted with a hand-made Candlewick bulb that looks uncannily like a conventional flame, and an ingenious beeswax candle cover which easily slips over a conventional wired socket. **3. The Saltbox** offers this handsome brass electric candlestick as part of its American Period collection. Fitted with a 7½-watt candelabra bulb, it is a classic style suitable for just about any decorating scheme.

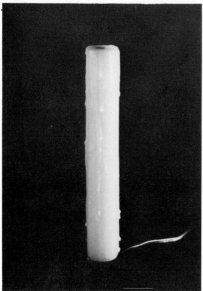

2

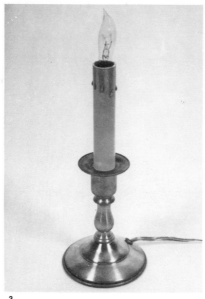

3

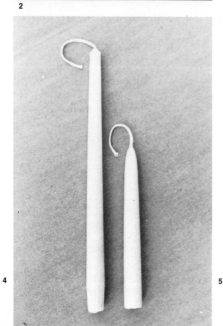

4

5

ELECTRIC LIGHT **IS NOW CHEAPER**

The new General Electric Tungsten Lamp gives nearly three times the light given by ordinary incandescent lamps.

General Electric Tungsten lamps make electric light available for many people who never before thought they could afford it.

General Electric
Tungsten Lamps

6

7

8

4, 5. If you're a stickler for the authentic period look, and the period is Colonial, you won't want to buy candles for your antique candlesticks in a local five and dime. **Hurley Patentee Lighting,** which creates superb 17th- and 18th-century reproductions, also sells beeswax candles in 7″ and 12″ sizes. For candelabras and wall sconces where an open flame is ill-advised, Hurley Patentee offers waxed candle sleeves, hand dripped and dipped, in 4″ and 6″ lengths. **6.** There could be nothing less appropriate than a 1980s electric light bulb illuminating an early 20th-century fixture. For that special vintage lamp, even when visibility is an issue, **Bradford Consultants** can supply classic bulbs like those first introduced between 1909 and 1930. As the old General Electric advertisement shows, these are Edison-type carbon loop filament bulbs which re-create the soft, mellow light of the early electric age. Bradford offers two different models, type "T" (1909-1920) and type "P" (1920-1930) of this bulb, which it calls the Eureka. Each can be used with a dimmer. **7, 8. William Spencer** offers several styles of solid-brass electric candles. Either of the two shown would look lovely placed in a window; the one on the right is small enough to fit on even the narrowest sill, as its base is a mere 2¼″ in diameter. Spencer offers this diminutive model in both 8″ and 5″ tall versions.

List of Suppliers

Mickey and Roberta Ackerman
Conversions
11 Sargent Ave.
Providence, RI 02906
(401) 831-7999

An excellent source for innovative one-of-a-kind lighting devices.

Art Directions
6120 Delmar Blvd.
St. Louis, MO 63112
(314) 863-1895

Wide collection of both antique and reproduction lighting fixtures for residential and municipal use.

Artemide Inc.
150 E. 58th St.
New York, NY 10155
(212) 980-0710

Catalogue available.

Trend-setting leader in Italian designs—the latest in contemporary lighting.

Authentic Designs
The Mill Rd.
West Rupert, VT 05776
(802) 394-7713

Catalogue, $3.

Handcrafted recreations and adaptations of early American lighting fixtures.

Authentic Lighting
558 Grand Ave.
Englewood, NJ 07631
(201) 568-7429

Repairs and refinishing of antique fixtures and accessories, including lamp shades.

Baldwin Giftware Corporation
841 Wyomissing Blvd.
Reading, PA 19603
(215) 777-7811

Catalogue available.

Authentic reproductions of brass fixtures and accessories from the colonial period.

Boyd Lighting Company
56 Twelfth St.
San Francisco, CA 94103
(415) 431-4300

Offers lighting fixtures ranging from precise historic reproductions to today's contemporary designs.

The Brass Knob
2309 18th St. N.W.
Washington, DC 20009
(202) 332-3370

Bountiful source of antique lighting including chandeliers, sconces, floor, and table lamps—rewired or simply "as is" if you want to try your hand at reconditioning.

Brass Light of Historic Walker's Point
719 S. 5th St.
Milwaukee, WI 53204
(414) 383-0675

Original Victorian fixtures such as gas, electric, and combination chandeliers and sconces can be found here; restoration is available.

Brasslight, Inc.
90 Main St.
Nyack, NY 10960
(914) 353-0567

Catalogue, $3.

Quality brass reproductions of Victorian and turn-of-the-century lighting.

Burdock Silk Lampshade Co.
11120 Roselle St., Suite G
San Diego, CA 92121
(619) 458-1005

Handsome Victorian silk shades for lamps of any size or design.

Calger Lighting, Inc.
200 Lexington Ave., Suite 801
New York, NY 10016
(212) 689-9511

Wide selection of traditional and modern lighting fixtures.

City Lights Antique Lighting
2226 Massachusetts Ave.
Cambridge, MA 02140
(617) 547-1490

Hard-to-find, solid brass floor lamps from the early electric period.

Citybarn Antiques
362 Atlantic Ave.
Brooklyn, NY 11217
(718) 855-8566

Offers a large selection of fixtures from 1850-1910; also has Art Deco and 1950s lights. Repair, rewiring, and refinishing available.

Classic Illumination
2743 Ninth St.
Berkeley, CA 94710
(415) 849-1842

Catalogue, $3.

A good source for fine, handcrafted reproduction lighting.

Conversions, *See* Ackerman.

Crawford's Old House Store
301 McCall St.
Waukesha, WI 53186
(414) 542-0685

Specializes in authentic reproductions of period-designed hardware, crystal-cut prisms for chandeliers, and lighting fixtures.

Cumberland General Store
Route 3
Crossville, TN 38555
(615) 484-8481

Catalogue, $3.75.

Charming country store that stocks anything and everything in the old-fashioned tradition; a source for period lighting.

Elcanco, Inc.
60 Chelmsford St.
Chelmsford, MA 01824
(617) 256-9972

Catalogue available.

Excellent source for handcrafted electric wax candles and flamelike bulbs for use in early American and Victorian lighting fixtures.

The Elegant Cat
1440 B St.
Eureka, CA 95501
(707) 445-0051

Brochure, $2.

Attractive selection of Victorian lamps and lamp shades.

The Essex Forge
13 Old Dennison Rd.
Essex, CT 06426
(203) 767-1808

Catalogue, $2.

True craftsmen working in the traditional New England style produce hand-wrought iron and tin fixtures.

Greg's Antique Lighting
12005 Wilshire Blvd.
Los Angeles, CA 90025
(213) 478-5475

An excellent source of original Victorian lighting fixtures rewired for electricity.

Half-Moon Antiques at Monmouth Antique Shoppes
217 W. Front St.
Red Bank, NJ 07701
(201) 842-1863

Expert restoration of antique lighting fixtures.

Hammerworks, *See* Lighting by Hammerworks.

Paul Hanson
610 Commercial Ave.
Carlstadt, NJ 07072
(201) 933-4873

Nationally known company with an extensive line of fixtures, ranging in style from Art Deco to contemporary.

Heinz & Co.
P.O. Box 663
Oak Park, IL 60303
(312) 383-1310

Makes superb reproductions of Frank Lloyd Wright's lighting designs.

House of Troy
P.O. Box 126
North Troy, VT 05859
(802) 988-2896

Specializes in hard-to-find picture, piano, and desk lamps.

Lyn Hovey Studio Inc.
266 Concord Ave.
Cambridge, MA 02138
(617) 492-6566

Catalogue, $2.

A talented staff of artists and specialists creates original stained glass designs and restores complex, delicate art glass pieces such as Tiffany and LaFarge windows.

Hubbardton Forge & Wood
RD 1
Fair Haven, VT 05743
(802) 273-2047

Catalogue, $2.

Skilled craftsmen create custom fixtures for any decorative or architectural need.

Humphrey Products
Kilgore at Sprinkle Rd.
P.O. Box 2008
Kalamazoo, MI 49003
(616) 381-5500

Brochure available.

Excellent source for energy-efficient propane gas lighting fixtures for indoor use.

Hurley Patentee Lighting
RD 7, Box 98A
Kingston, NY 12401
(914) 331-5414

Catalogue, $2.

Faithful reproductions of lamps,
sconces, and chandeliers from the
17th and 18th centuries.

Illuminating Experiences, Inc.
107 Trumbull St.
Elizabeth, NJ 07206
(201) 527-8847

Catalogue, $5.

Versatile lighting fixtures ranging
from colonial and Victorian
reproductions to Art Deco and
postmodern designs.

Interna Designs, Ltd.
The Merchandise Mart
Space 6-168
Chicago, IL 60654
(312) 467-6076

Exclusive distributor of some of the
best and most up-to-date Italian
lighting fixtures.

IPI—Innovative Products for
  Interiors Inc.
315 E. 62nd St.
New York, NY 10021
(212) 838-2900

Distributor of distinctive modern
lighting designs.

Steve Kayne & Son
76 Daniel Ridge Rd.
Candler, NC 28715
(704) 667-8868

Catalogue of hand-forged hard-
ware, $2.
Catalogue of colonial hardware, $2.
Both catalogues, $3.

Family-owned custom hardware
shop; offers handmade fixtures.

Ray King
603 S. 10th St.
Philadelphia, PA 19147
(215) 627-5112

An ingenious craftsman who
creates one-of-a-kind lighting fixtures for innovation-loving clients.

Koch & Lowy Inc.
21-24 39th Ave.
Long Island City, NY 11101
(212) 786-3520

Catalogue, $5.

Fine quality traditional and contemporary lighting.

George Kovacs Lighting, Inc.
24 W. 40th St.
New York, NY 10018
(212) 944-9606

Catalogue, $2.

An excellent source of traditional
and modern fixtures.

John Kruesel's General Merchandise and Auction Co.
22 3rd St. S.W.
Rochester, MN 55902
(507) 289-8049

Original period lighting, from
candles and whale oil lamps to
kerosene, gas, electric, and combination fixtures.

Lazin Lighting Inc.
23 Second Ave.
New York, NY 10003
(212) 219-3888

Innovative modern lighting fixtures.

Joe Ley Antiques, Inc.
615 E. Market St.
Louisville, KY 40202
(502) 583-4014

Offers a large selection of antique
fixtures—crystal, bronze, glass, and
brass.

Lighting by Hammerworks
75 Webster St.
Worcester, MA 01603
(617) 755-3434

Catalogue, $2.

Handcrafted lighting fixtures inspired by the best styles of
yesteryear.

Lightworks
3345 West Hunting Park Ave.
Philadelphia, PA 19132
(215) 223-9200

Manufactures and distributes tube
lighting and other forms of lineal
light for application in the home or
in a commercial setting.

The London Venturers Company
2 Dock Square
Rockport, MA 01966
(617) 546-7161

Antique lighting restoration and
rewiring.

Materials Unlimited
2 W. Michigan Ave.
Ypsilanti, MI 48197
(313) 483-6980

Brochure, $3.

An extensive collection of antique
fixtures; this is an excellent source
for hard-to-find items.

Mark McDonnell
12 Rhode Island Ave.
Providence, RI 02906
(401) 331-2958

An artisan whose work has been ex-
hibited in many museums and art
galleries, McDonnell creates
beautiful hand-blown glass table
lamps and sconces.

Metropolitan Lighting Fixture
  Co. Inc.
1010 Third Ave.
New York, NY 10021
(212) 838-2425

Catalogue, $5.

Offers an extensive line of
reproductions of both turn-of-the-
century fixtures and more contemporary designs.

M-H Lamp & Fan Company
7231½ N. Sheridan Rd.
Chicago, IL 60626
(312) 743-2225

Catalogue, $3.

Manufacturers of solid-brass Victorian and early 20th-century
fixtures.

Mill River Hammerworks
65 Canal St.
Turners Falls, MA 01376
(413) 863-8388

Custom hand-wrought metal work
and repair and restoration services;
all items are made to order.

Gates Moore
River Rd., Silvermine
RD-3
Norwalk, CT 06850
(203) 847-3231

Catalogue, $2.

A fine source for handcrafted early
American-style fixtures.

Museum of Modern Art
The Museum Store
11 West 53rd St.
New York, NY 10019
(212) 708-9888

Catalogue, $2.

Selections from the best designs in
this world-renowned museum's permanent collection are chosen to be
reproduced in the retail shop, including some of its superb lighting
devices.

Nessen Lamps Inc.
621 E. 216th St.
Bronx, NY 10467
(212) 231-0221

Some of best contemporary lighting
designs.

Newstamp Lighting
227 Bay Rd.
N. Easton, MA 02356
(617) 238-7071

A family-owned-and-operated
business specializing in custom
lanterns and other antique fixtures
made to exact specifications.

Nowell's Inc.
490 Gate Five Rd.
Sausalito, CA 94966
(415) 332-4933

Catalogue, $3.50.

Reproduction lighting fixtures and
museum-quality restoration of antique lighting devices.

Old Lamplighter Shop at the
  Musical Museum
Deansboro, NY 13328
(315) 841-8774

Specializes in old lamps, lamp
parts, repairs, and restorations, and
carries a wide range of accessories.

Period Furniture Hardware
  Co., Inc.
123 Charles St.
P.O. Box 314, Charles St. Station
Boston, MA 02114
(617) 227-0758

Catalogue, $3.50 U.S., $5.00
  Canada

Reproduces numerous light fixtures
from the colonial era.

Plexability
Suite 506
New York Design Center
200 Lexington Ave.
New York, NY 10016
(212) 679-7826

Catalogue available.

Sleek, ultramodern lighting fixtures
made of acrylic.

Price-Glover Antiques
817½ Madison Ave.
New York, NY 10021
(212) 772-1740

Catalogue available.

Excellent source for 18th-century
and Victorian antiques and exceptional reproductions.

Progress Lighting
Erie Ave. and G St.
Philadelphia, PA 19134
(215) 289-1200

Catalogue, $3.

One of the nation's largest
manufacturers of lighting fixtures,
in styles ranging from colonial
reproductions to today's contemporary designs.

Roy Electric Co. Inc.
1054 Coney Island Ave.
Brooklyn, NY 11230
(212) 339-6311

Catalogue available.

This company specializes in restoring and reproducing large, elaborate
Victorian chandeliers for ballrooms,
restaurants, and hotels, but its
craftsmen welcome commissions in
smaller sizes as well.

Hap Sakwa
1330 8th St.
Baywood Park, CA 93402
(805) 528-7585

An artisan who exhibits unlimited
creativity in the area of contemporary lighting.

The Saltbox
2229 Marietta Pike
Lancaster, PA 17603
(717) 392-5649

Brochure, $1.

The home of American Period Lighting Fixtures, this shop produces designs of the 1800s; its craftsmen work with antique tools to create authentic reproductions by hand.

Gail H. Teller
The Shade Tree
6 Half-King Dr.
Burlington, CT 06013
(203) 673-9358

Catalogue, $1.

Specializes in handcrafted cut and pierced lamp shades; designs can be ordered from stock, or shades can be made to individual specifications.

Shades of the Past
P.O. Box 502
Corte Madera, CA 94925
(415) 459-6999

Brochure, $3.

Tracy Holcomb is the artist, designer, and craftsman behind the re-creations of exuberant turn-of-the-century silk lamp shades and brass bases.

Shaker Workshops
P.O. Box 1028
Concord, MA 01742
(617) 646-8985

Catalogue, $1.

Can supply either do-it-yourself kits or already assembled lighting fixtures reproduced from original Shaker designs.

Sierra Trading Company
1836 Old Ione Rd. #4
Martell, CA 95654
(209) 223-0886

Catalogue, $1.

Fine source for Moire-style and Gallé reproduction lamps, in addition to chandeliers and fixtures.

William Spencer, Inc.
Creek Rd.
Rancocas Woods, NJ 08060
(609) 235-1830

Catalogue, $2.

A family-owned business, established in 1897, manufactures hundreds of fixtures; styles range from colonial to Victorian.

Spring City Elect. Mfg. Co.
P.O. Drawer A
Spring City, PA 19475
(215) 948-4000

Brochure available.

An excellent source of cast-iron posts for outdoor fixtures.

Karl Springer Ltd.
306 E. 61st St.
New York, NY 10021
(212) 752-1695

Though this company specializes in fine leather furniture, it has recently introduced an assortment of Venetian glass lighting fixtures.

Stanley Galleries Antiques
2118 North Clark St.
Chicago, IL 60614
(312) 281-1614

Brochure available.

Specializes in original restored American antique lighting fixtures, circa 1850-1940; no reproductions are carried.

Squaw Alley, Inc.
401 S. Main St.
Naperville, IL 60540
(312) 357-0200

Catalogue, $3.

Offers both antique and reproduction chandeliers, sconces, and lamps in a variety of styles.

Turn of the Century Lighting
118 Sherbourne St.
Toronto, Canada M5A 2R2
(416) 362-6203

Offers a wide selection of diverse lighting styles, including Victorian, Eastlake, Art Nouveau, Mission, and Art Deco; also offers a comprehensive repair and restoration service.

Uplift Inc.
506 Hudson St.
New York, NY 10014
(212) 929-3632

Specializes in hard-to-find Art Deco fixtures and stocks the largest supply of Depression-era lighting devices on the East Coast.

Victorian Lightcrafters Ltd.
P.O. Box 350
Slate Hill, NY 10973
(914) 355-1300

Catalogue, $3.

Restores and sells antique lighting and also has its own line of reproduction fixtures.

Victorian Lighting Works
The Gamble Mill
160 Dunlop St.
Bellefonte, PA 16823
(814) 355-8449

A fine collection of Victorian reproduction chandeliers, wall sconces, and glass shades.

Victorian Reproductions, Inc.
1601 Park Ave. S.
Minneapolis, MN 55404
(612) 338-3636

Brochure, $1.50.
Catalogue, $4.

A collection of re-created styles from the 1800s to the 1920s can be found here.

E. G. Washburne & Co.
85 Andover St. Rt. 114
Danvers, MA 01923
(617) 774-3645

Brochure available.

Specializes in authentic reproduction lanterns; models include wall, post, and free-standing fixtures.

The Washington Copper Works
Serge Miller, Proprietor
Washington, CT 06793
(203) 868-7527

Catalogue, $3.

Each copper fixture made by Serge Miller or one of his apprentices is initialed and dated, a testament to the quality of their hand-wrought work.

Beth Weissman
260 Smith St.
Farmingdale, NY 11735
(516) 694-7950

Catalogues available.

This 63-year-old firm is best known for its quality traditional lamps, but its collection includes contemporary designs from France, Italy, and Germany.

Welsbach Lighting, Inc.
240 Sargent Dr.
New Haven, CT 06511
(203) 789-1710

Catalogue available.

An extensive line of Victorian outdoor lighting products; Welsbach is a pioneer in producing functioning gas fixtures.

Lt. Moses Willard & Company
7805 Railroad Ave.
Cincinnati, OH 45243
(513) 561-3942

Catalogue, $2.

This group of tincrafters specializes in recreating the intricate beauty of metal designs of the past, such as chandeliers, wall sconces, and lanterns.

The Wrecking Bar of Atlanta, Inc.
292 Moreland Ave. N.E.
Atlanta, GA 30307
(404) 525-0468

Brochure available.

A continually changing supply of antique fixtures for many different purposes.

Yankee Craftsman
357 Commonwealth Rd. (Rt. 30)
Wayland, MA 01778
(617) 653-0031

Bill Sweeney and his sons are among the country's foremost antique lighting restorers; they also have a very extensive collection of gas, oil, and early electric fixtures for sale.

Yestershades
3534 S.E. Hawthorne
Portland, OR 97214
(503) 238-5755

Catalogue, $3.50

Esther Rister and her staff make colorful silk lamp shades reminiscent of those popular in the early 1900s.